Women of the Old Testament

14 In-Depth Bible Studies for Teens
with Mother-Daughter Discussion Starters

Barbara Frank

Answer key included

CARDAMOM PUBLISHERS
JANESVILLE, WI

Women of the Old Testament, 14 In-Depth Bible Studies for Teens
Copyright © 2010 Barbara Frank/Cardamom Publishers
All rights reserved

Published by
Cardamom Publishers
P.O. Box 2146
Janesville, WI 53547

Printed in the United States of America

ISBN 978-0-9742181-5-1
Library of Congress Control Number: 2010904508

Library of Congress Subject Heading: 1. Home schooling--Biblical teaching.
2. Bible study for women.
3. Bible Teenagers' use.
4. Home schooling--Curricula.

Dedication

To Mary Charlotte Frank: "For this child I prayed."

Contents

How to Use This Book

I've used Bible study curricula from several different publishers while homeschooling my children. I always wanted to write my own, but never found the time until my third child reached her early teens. That's when I finally wrote this Bible curriculum about the best-known women of the Old Testament.

Like many Bible studies, this book includes questions and an answer key. However, it's different from most Bible studies because part of it requires your participation as well as your daughter's.

Each study has three sections. The first section consists of questions that lead your daughter through the Bible story methodically, asking for specific details that can be found through careful reading. I used this format so that my daughter would pick up many of the details she might otherwise miss in a cursory reading of the text.

The second section, "Short Essay Questions," helped my daughter think about the story she had just read, details and all, and come to some conclusions about it.

Our favorite section was the third section, "Discussion Starters for Mothers and Daughters." We usually set aside a specific time for just the two of us after she finished studying each Bible story. I thought up the discussion starters to help me relate aspects of each story to my own life. My daughter loved hearing about my experiences, and I enjoyed sharing them with her. Thanks to these discussions, we learned a lot about each other, and drew even closer in the process. I encourage you to add experiences of your own, should they occur to you, to keep each discussion going.

If you're not familiar with these Bible stories, you'll want to read each one before doing the related discussion starters with your daughter. You might also want to read the discussion starters a day or two ahead of time so you have time to think about them; this helps bring back memories you can share with your daughter.

Some of the topics discussed in this study are appropriate for teens but not younger girls, so the recommended age range is 13 and up.

You can assign this book any way you like. I usually assigned one or two pages of questions daily, correcting them as my daughter completed them (the answer key is included in the back; its pages have a solid side border to make the key easy to find.) After she finished the questions, I'd assign her the short essay questions for one or more days' work. Once we'd gone over those, we'd take time out to sit and chat about the discussion starters, sometimes over a cup of hot chocolate and a sweet snack.

At the beginning of each group of questions, you'll see this symbol:

 _3/29_

You can write an assignment date next to the flower on each blank so your daughter will know which day you want her to do the work. If she's working through the book more informally, she can write down the dates as she goes along, making the book more like a journal.

The "Short Essay Questions" also add to the "journal feel" of this book. I loved reading my daughter's essay question answers when I recently re-read our original version of this book during the publishing process. She's currently a college student, so it's been five years since she wrote those answers. Reading them again revealed her spiritual growth over the past five years and also brought back wonderful memories of the young girl she used to be.

Your daughter can use any translation of the Bible that you prefer with this book. I used the King James Version (KJV) and New International Version (NIV) when I wrote it; please keep that in mind when you correct the answers. The answer key occasionally quotes directly from the KJV or NIV, so a specific quote might be different in another translation. When in doubt, use your best judgment.

If you choose to grade your daughter's work, just keep track of the percentage of correct answers in each section, and average them out at the end of the grading period.

I hope this Bible curriculum is a blessing to your daughter... and to you!

Barbara Frank
March 2010

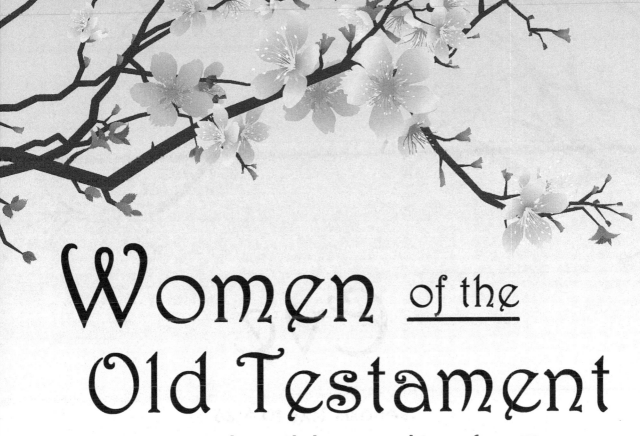

Women of the Old Testament

14 In-Depth Bible Studies for Teens
with Mother-Daughter Discussion Starters

Eve

Genesis 1:26 to 4:26
Time Period: Creation

In this section, you will learn about Eve: how she came to be, what she did and what happened to her, and how God showed He loved her.

 Read Genesis 1:26-31, then answer the following questions:

1. Who was with God in the beginning? (Note the reference to "us" in verse 26.) Also, look up John 1:1-2 for the answer.

2. Who created male and female, and in whose image were they created?

3. What did God do to them?

4.   What three things did He tell them to do?

5.   Did He tell Adam, Eve or both of them?

6.   What does it mean to increase in number?

7.   What did God give Adam and Eve for food?

Read Genesis 2:1-25

8.   How did God form Adam?

9.   How did Adam come to life?

10. What place did God provide for Adam to live in?

11. Where was this place?

12. What did God provide there for Adam's survival?

13. What two items were in the middle of the garden?

Eve

14. What was Adam's job?

15. What was God's command to Adam?

16. What would happen if Adam disobeyed the command?

17. What did God say Adam needed?

18. What did God and Adam do next?

19. Was a helper found for Adam?

20. Explain how Adam received a helper.

21. What was the helper called?

22. Who named her that?

23. When Adam said, "This is now bone of my bones and flesh of my flesh," what did he mean?

24. In what ceremony is verse 24 often cited?

25. Why?

26. Why weren't Adam and Eve ashamed to be naked? (verse 25)

———— Read Genesis 3:1-7

27. What was the craftiest of the wild animals God made?

28. What did the serpent say to the woman?

29. How did the woman answer the serpent?

30. What did the serpent do then?

31. What did the woman do after that?

32. Did the serpent force her to eat the apple?

33. What happened once the woman and Adam ate the fruit?

Eve

34. Go back and re-read Gen. 2: 15-17. Who did God command not to eat from the tree of the knowledge of good and evil?

35. Since the woman knew what God had said about not eating from the tree of the knowledge of good and evil, Adam must have told her what God said. Which of them, Adam or the woman, was responsible for their disobedience?

36. The serpent (Satan) used temptation to get the woman to disobey God. Does God ever use temptation to test us and see if we really will obey him? Look up James 1:13 for help.

Read Genesis 3:8-24

37. What did they hear in the garden?

38. What did they do?

39. Why did they do that? What caused their fear?

40. Had they been afraid of Him before?

41. Who answered God when He called out 'Where are you?'?"

42. How did that person answer God?

43. Even though God knew right away that Adam and the woman had eaten from the tree, He asked Adam anyway. Why?

44. Who did Adam blame for this disobedience?

45. Who did the woman blame for this disobedience?

46. Who deserves the blame for this disobedience?

47. What were the consequences of this sin for the serpent?

48. In verse 15, God tells the serpent He will put enmity between the serpent and the woman, between its offspring (seed) and hers. Look up the word "enmity" and write the definition here:

Who is the woman's offspring (seed)? (See Galatians 3:16 for a clue)

Who is the serpent's offspring (seed)? (See Revelation 12:9 for a clue)

Eve

49. Verse 15 quotes God as saying to the serpent, "...he will crush your head, and you will strike his heel." Look up Romans 16:20; what does God mean?

50. What were the consequences of this sin for the woman?

51. What were the consequences of this sin for Adam?

52. What does God mean when he says, "...for dust you are and to dust you will return"?

53. Who chose the woman's name, and what did he name her?

54. Why did he name her that?

55. We have all descended from the woman, but who is her most important descendant?

56. Adam and Eve disobeyed God, so they had to suffer the consequences of their behavior. Yet God still loved them. How did He show it?

57. Remember from Gen. 2:9 that there were two trees: 1) the tree of life,

and 2) the tree of the knowledge of good and evil. Since Adam and Eve ate from the second tree, what does God say about the first tree in Gen. 3:22?

58. What did God do then?

59. What did God put at the entrance to the garden and why?

Read Genesis 4:1-16

60. When Adam and Eve had their first child, Cain, whom did Eve credit with Cain's creation?

61. What was their next child's name?

62. Adam and Eve's family suffered the consequences of the sin that came into the world because of their disobedient act in the garden. Briefly explain what happened between Cain and Abel.

63. How did God show He still loved Cain?

64. Although Eve lost her first two sons, God blessed her with at least one more; see Gen. 4:25 to find his name.

Eve

Short Essay Questions

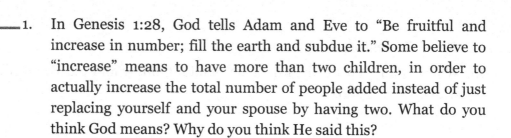

You're encouraged to use a concordance to find Bible verses that will help you answer these questions. For example, in question 1, looking up words like "fruitful," "children," and "multiply" will lead you to verses that will guide you as you answer the question.

1. In Genesis 1:28, God tells Adam and Eve to "Be fruitful and increase in number; fill the earth and subdue it." Some believe to "increase" means to have more than two children, in order to actually increase the total number of people added instead of just replacing yourself and your spouse by having two. What do you think God means? Why do you think He said this?

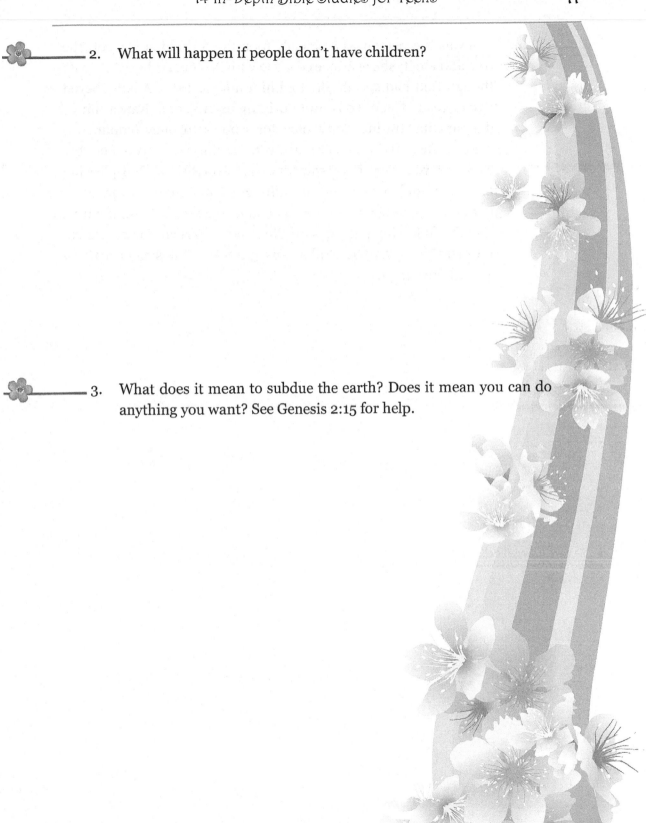

2. What will happen if people don't have children?

3. What does it mean to subdue the earth? Does it mean you can do anything you want? See Genesis 2:15 for help.

Eve

4. Eve was the person who actually took the forbidden fruit off the tree and ate it; she also shared some with Adam and he ate it, even though God had specifically told him not to. Thus, Adam obeyed Eve instead of God. Look up 1 Corinthians 11:3, and draw a simple diagram illustrating God's plan for who is to obey (submit to) whom. Then write a short essay describing how you and the husband you may have someday can establish a God-pleasing marriage, and how it will be different from Adam's and Eve's relationship, as shown in the incident of the serpent and the tree. Use the following passages on Christian marriage for guidance: 1 Corinthians 7:10-11, Ephesians 5:22-32, Colossians 3:18-19 and 1 Peter 3:1-7.

5. Did the serpent come right out and tell Eve to eat the fruit? No;
    instead he discredited God's authority, confused and tempted Eve,
    and told her she'd be like God. How does Satan do that to us
    sometimes? Give an example of when this has happened to you,
    and how you can avoid it the next time it happens. (Clue: read
    James 4:7, and Matthew 4:8-11, 7:7-8.)

Eve

 6. The serpent tempted Eve by telling her that if she ate the fruit, she would become like God. Why would someone want to become like God?

 7. Even though Eve sinned against God, He still loved her, and allowed her to become the mother of all future humans, including (and especially) Jesus. What an honor to be a great-great-.......great-grandmother of Jesus! Write about a time when God blessed you despite the times you've disobeyed Him.

8. It's tempting for us to criticize Adam and Eve for disobeying God and causing sin to come into the world. Look up and read John 8:7 and Luke 6:41-42, then write what Jesus says about our willingness to criticize others for their sins. What does this mean for you?

9. Imagine you're Eve. After a peaceful and comfortable life in the Garden of Eden, with God as a regular visitor, you and Adam have now been sent away because of your disobedience. What are you thinking and feeling?

Eve

Discussion Starters for Mothers and Daughters

Read Matthew 19:3-6; why did Jesus quote Genesis 2:24? Is that concern still an issue today?

Given God's definition of marriage in Genesis 2:24, can a couple be married if neither is a woman? What if neither is a man?

In Genesis 3:15, God tells the serpent, "I will put enmity between you and the woman, and between your offspring and hers; he will crush your head, and you will strike his heel." What's worse, to have your head crushed, or your heel struck? Equate these two events to what would eventually happen to the offspring of the serpent and Eve.

Notes:

Eve

Sarah

Genesis 11:27 to 23:20
Time Period: 2100-2050 BC

In this section you'll learn about Sarah, a beautiful woman whose marriage and motherhood was used by God to teach her many things.

 Read Genesis 11:27-32, then answer the following questions:

1. What was the name of Abram's wife?

2. What do you learn about her in verse 30?

3. Where did Terah take his family, including Sarai?

Read Genesis 12:1-9

4. What did the Lord tell Abram to do?

5. What did God promise Abram He would do?

6. Did Abram obey God?

7. How old was Abram at this time?

8. How old do you think Sarai was at this time?

9. Where did Abram and his family go after the Lord spoke to him?

10. Once there, what did God promise Abram?

11. Did Abram have offspring?

12. What did God's promise imply?

Sarah

Read Genesis 12:10 to 13:2

13. Why did Abram and Sarai leave Canaan to go to Egypt?

14. What did Abram warn Sarai about just before they entered Egypt?

15. What was he really asking her to do?

16. What did the Egyptians think when they first saw Sarai?

17. Where was Sarai taken?

18. What did Pharaoh give to Abram after bringing Sarai to his palace?

19. Why did Pharaoh do that?

20. What did God to do Pharaoh's household because of Sarai?

21. Why?

22. Why didn't God let Sarai remain at the palace?

23. What did Pharaoh do after God punished him and his household?

24. Where did Abram and Sarai go from Egypt?

25. What does verse 2 tell us about Abram?

26. How did he get that way?

Read Genesis 15:1-6

27. Who came to visit Abram in a vision?

28. How did Abram respond?

29. What was the first promise Abram was given?

30. What was the second promise Abram was given?

31. Did Abram believe these promises?

32. What would the promises mean for Sarai? (Hint: read Psalm 113:9.)

Sarah

Read Genesis 16:1-15

33. What was the name of Sarai's maidservant?

34. What did Sarai ask Abram to do with Hagar?

35. Why did Sarai do this?

36. Did Abram agree to Sarai's plan?

37. What happened to Hagar?

38. How did Hagar behave after that?

39. Why did Hagar act that way?

40. How did Sarai respond to Hagar's behavior?

41. What was Abram's response to Sarai's complaint?

42. What did Sarai do to Hagar?

43. What did Hagar do then?

44. Who found Hagar?

45. What did he tell Hagar to do?

46. What did he promise Hagar?

47. What did he tell her would be happening soon?

48. What did Hagar call God?

49. What happened to Hagar in verse 15?

50. How old was Abram when this happened?

Read Genesis 17:1-14

In this passage, the Lord again appears to Abram, now 99 years old, and confirms the covenant, which was hinted at in chapter 12 and first mentioned in chapter 15. God tells Abram he will have many, many descendants, and that Canaan will belong to them. He changes Abram's name (which means "exalted father") to Abraham ("father of many"), and

Sarah

tells him He will make him very fruitful. Since Abraham is already the father of Ishmael, this can only mean God will send more children to Abraham.

Read Genesis 17:15-22

51. What did God tell Abraham to call his wife?

52. What plans did God have for Sarah?

53. How did Abraham react to God's words?

54. Why did Abraham react in this way?

55. What was God's response?

56. According to verse 21, when would this event occur?

Read Genesis 18:1-15

57. Who arrived at Abraham's tent?

58. It was the custom in those times to be hospitable to strangers. What did Abraham tell Sarah to do?

59. As Abraham ate with his guests, what did they ask him?

60. Read verse 10 carefully. Who does the Bible say spoke? Who were these men and where did they come from?

61. What message was given to Abraham?

62. Sarah was behind the messenger, listening. How did she react to the message?

63. Who knew what Sarah was thinking to herself?

64. How did He respond to Sarah's laughter?

65. How did Sarah feel then?

66. What did she do next?

67. How did He respond to that?

Sarah

Read Genesis 20:1-18

68. What mistake from his past did Abraham repeat?

69. What did Abraham's statement make Abimelech, king of Gerar, think it was permissible to do?

70. How did God protect Sarah?

71. How did Abimelech respond?

72. What did God tell Abimelech He had done?

73. What did God tell Abimelech to do?

74. Where did the conversation between God and Abimelech occur?

75. What did Abimelech do after talking to God?

76. How did Abraham respond?

77. What did Abimelech do to Abraham?

78. How did Abraham respond?

Read Genesis 21:1-7

79. What promise to Sarah did God fulfill?

80. According to verse 2, when did this happen?

81. How did Abraham obey God in verse 3?

82. How did Abraham obey God in verse 4?

83. How old was Abraham when this happened?

84. Remember that Sarah laughed when she was told this was going to happen. How did she respond once it did happen, and how was it different?

Read Genesis 21:8-12

85. Define "wean." What did Abraham do when Isaac was weaned?

86. Whose behavior upset Sarah at the feast?

Sarah

87. What did Sarah tell Abraham to do?

88. How did Abraham feel about this? Why?

89. What did God tell Abraham to do?

90. What did God say about Ishmael?

Read Genesis 23:1-2

91. How old did Sarah live to be?

92. How did Abraham react to Sarah's death?

93. With approximately how many years of motherhood did God bless Sarah? For help, go back to question 54.

Short Essay Questions

1. Genesis 11:30 tells us that Sarai was barren, meaning she was unable to have children. In the time in which she lived, being barren was believed to be a punishment from God. (Note that in Genesis 20:17-18, God prevented Abimelech and his family from having children: He literally "closed up every womb in Abimelech's household.") Although there are medical treatments today that help some barren women have children, there are other women who still cannot have any. Do you believe barrenness is a punishment from God? Can you think of any other reasons why God might not give a woman a child?

Sarah

 2. We're told in the Bible that Sarai was beautiful. Our society places a great emphasis on beauty. We can all appreciate beauty, but what does God say about beauty in the Bible in the following verses?

Proverbs 31:30

Matthew 23:27-28

 3. Re-read Genesis 12:11-20, then describe what bad things would not have happened if Sarai had not been beautiful.

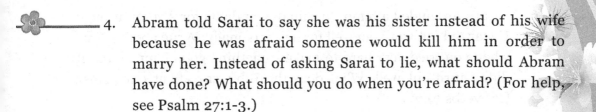

4. Abram told Sarai to say she was his sister instead of his wife because he was afraid someone would kill him in order to marry her. Instead of asking Sarai to lie, what should Abram have done? What should you do when you're afraid? (For help, see Psalm 27:1-3.)

5. In Genesis 16:1-2, Sarai asked Abram to sleep with her maidservant Hagar in hopes that Hagar would then have a child, thus making God's promise of offspring for Abram come true. Must God have human help to fulfill His promises? Give some examples from the Bible to support your answer.

Sarah

 6. Sarai's misguided attempt to gain descendants for Abram through Hagar did not work out well for her personally. Write about a time when you tried very hard to make something good happen, but it didn't turn out well. What does the Bible say about our plans? (Proverbs 19:21)

 7. It was Sarai's idea for Hagar to bear a child for Abram, yet Sarai mistreated Hagar and caused her to run away. Why did Sarai mistreat Hagar? Can you think of a time when you got your way but it ended up making you unhappy?

8. After Sarah heard the visitor's message that she would have a son, she laughed to herself, then denied doing it when the Lord asked why she laughed. Is there ever a time when God does not know our thoughts? How is it that He knows us so well? Why did He ask, "Is anything too hard for the Lord?"

9. As a godly wife, Sarah was expected to obey her husband Abraham. So when he asked her to lie, not once but twice, so others would think she was only Abraham's sister and not his wife, she did so. God used both these situations for good, but Sarah wouldn't have known that at the time. If you were Sarah, would you have obeyed him? Why or why not?

Sarah

 _____ 10. Read Hebrews 11. This chapter describes some of God's people throughout history who were blessed with faith. In verse 11, the writer (we don't know who it was) could have simply said that Abraham's wife was barren, but instead referred to her by name. In fact, Sarah was one of only two women mentioned by name in that "Faith Hall of Fame;" the rest of the people listed there were men. Who was the other woman, and what else did these two women have in common? (For a clue, read Matthew 1:1-17.)

 _____ 11. Read Genesis 22:1-18. Given what you've learned about Sarah in this Bible study, use that knowledge to answer this question: *If Sarah knew why Abraham took Isaac to Moriah (we aren't told whether she knew or not), do you think she tried to stop him? Would you if you were Sarah?*

Discussion Starters for Mothers and Daughters

Sarah grew impatient waiting for the promised offspring, so she urged Abram to father a child with her maidservant Hagar. We, too, can be impatient at times for God's will to be done. Why is it sinful for us to try to make His will happen in our timing?

Sarah expressed great joy at the long-awaited birth of her son Isaac. Describe to your daughter the story of her arrival and how much joy you felt when it happened.

Although Sarah obeyed her husband Abraham, even when he told her to lie about being his wife, she was still willing to give Abraham her opinions. In Genesis 21:12, God even told Abraham to "listen to whatever Sarah tells you because it is through Isaac that your offspring will be reckoned." Use this to talk about how a husband and wife should talk to each other, where

Sarah

obedience comes in, and how each should behave toward the other. Verses that will help you include: 1 Corinthians 11:3, Ephesians 5:22-33, Colossians 3:18-19, and 1 Peter 3:1.

Notes:

Sarah

Rebekah

Genesis 24 to 35:29
Time Period: 2030-1960 BC

Rebekah is the story of the young woman who married Isaac, the son of Abraham and Sarah. As the wife of Isaac and the daughter-in-law of Abraham, she would be part of God's fulfillment of His promise to Abraham that he would be "the father of many nations."

 Read Genesis 24:1-14, then answer the following questions:

1. Abraham wanted his son Isaac to marry, but he did not want him to marry a woman from what group?

2. Abraham told his servant to find a wife for Isaac from among what group of people?

3. What was the servant worried about?

4. Did Abraham want Isaac to go with the servant? Why or why not?

5. Who would be going on the trip with the servant, according to Abraham?

6. What would happen if the servant found a woman who did not want to come back to Canaan?

7. What did the servant take with him on his journey?

8. To what town did the servant go?

9. What was the first thing he did when he got there?

10. What was the second thing he did when he got there? Be specific.

Read Genesis 24:15-27

11. What happened before Abraham's servant could finish praying at the spring?

Rebekah

12. How was Rebekah related to Isaac? (Draw a diagram if you like.)

13. How is Rebekah described in verse 16?

14. What did the servant say to Rebekah?

15. How did she respond to the servant?

16. What items did the servant take out that he had brought with him?

17. What two questions did the servant then ask Rebekah?

18. Why did he ask her the first question?

19. How did the servant thank God?

Read Genesis 24:28-49

20. What did Rebekah do after the servant said God had led him there?

21. Who came out to meet the servant?

22. Why did he come out?

23. What did he do for the servant?

24. Why didn't the servant want to eat right away?

Read Genesis 24:50-61

25. What question did the servant ask Rebekah's family after he told them how he came to be with them?

26. Who answered the question, and what was the answer?

27. What did the servant do once they had answered him?

28. In the morning, the servant was ready to take Rebekah and leave for Canaan, but her brother and her mother had a request of him. What was it?

29. Did the servant grant their request?

30. When they requested the same thing of Rebekah, how did she respond?

Rebekah

31. Who accompanied Rebekah and the servant on their trip to Canaan?

32. What did Rebekah's family do when she was ready to leave?

Read Genesis 24:62-67

33. Where had Isaac come from?

34. Why did he go out into the field?

35. He saw camels approaching; who was with the camels?

36. What did Rebekah do when she found out it was Isaac walking towards her?

37. After the servant told Isaac where he had been and why, what did Isaac do?

38. After that, how did Isaac feel about Rebekah?

39. How was God already using Rebekah in Isaac's life?

Read Genesis 25:19-26

40. How old was Isaac when he married Rebekah?

41. Once they were married, why did Isaac have to pray on behalf of Rebekah?

42. What happened as a result of his prayer?

43. What happened that made Rebekah decide to inquire of the Lord?

44. What was God's answer to her question?

45. Describe what happened in verses 24 to 26.

46. How old was Isaac when this occurred?

47. How long had he waited for an answer to his prayer on behalf of Rebekah?

 Read Genesis 25:27-34

48. Describe Esau and Jacob, according to verse 27.

Rebekah

49. How did Rebekah and Isaac feel about Esau and Jacob?

50. When Esau came home hungry one day and asked Jacob for some of the stew he was cooking, what was Jacob's response?

51. How did Esau react to Jacob's response?

52. Jacob made Esau do something else before he gave him some stew; what did he require of Esau?

53. What did Jacob then give Esau to eat?

54. Once Esau ate and drank, he left. What does the Bible say about Esau's behavior?

Read Genesis 26:1-11

55. What natural disaster struck the land Isaac and Rebekah lived in?

56. Isaac went to King Abimelech in Gerar for help; while he was there, what did God tell him to do?

57. Did Isaac obey God?

58. When the men in Gerar asked him about Rebekah, how did Isaac respond?

59. Why did he give that response?

60. To what other husband and wife in the Old Testament did this happen (twice)?

61. Did the situation work out differently for Isaac and Rebekah than it did for the other husband and wife?

62. How did God use this situation for good?

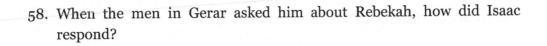 **Read Genesis 26:12-13**

63. What did God do for Isaac and Rebekah that solved the problem of the famine?

64. What was the end result for Isaac and Rebekah?

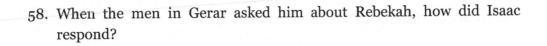 **Read Genesis 26:34-35**

65. How old was Esau when he got married?

Rebekah

66. Whom did Esau marry?

67. How did Isaac and Rebekah feel about their daughters-in-law?

Read Genesis 27:1-13

68. Why did Isaac call for Esau?

69. What did he ask Esau to do?

70. Who was listening to their conversation?

71. How did the listener react to Isaac's request of Esau?

72. Why do you think Jacob was told to get goats, instead of wild game?

73. Did Jacob understand what his mother really wanted him to do? Provide proof for your answer.

74. What did Jacob fear would happen?

75. How did his mother reassure him?

Read Genesis 27:13-29

76. What did Jacob and Rebekah do in an effort to secure Isaac's blessing on Jacob?

77. Who got to Isaac first, Esau or Jacob?

78. How did the son who got there first identify himself to his father Isaac?

79. Since Isaac was blind (see verse 1), what did he do to see if the son in front of him was Esau?

80. Could Isaac tell which son it was by touching him?

81. What did Isaac do in an effort to make sure it was Esau with him?

82. What did Isaac do once he was told it was Esau in front of him?

83. When his son kissed him, how did Isaac react to the smell of his clothes?

84. What kind of good things did Isaac say he wanted God to give his son?

Rebekah

Read Genesis 27:30-40

85. Who came in from hunting and prepared tasty food for his father?

86. What did he say to his father after bringing him the food?

87. How did his father Isaac respond?

88. After Esau identified himself, how did Isaac react physically?

89. What did Isaac then reveal to Esau?

90. What did Esau do after Isaac's revelation?

91. Isaac then identified the person to whom he had given the blessing. Who was it, and what did Isaac say about him?

92. Isaac didn't know it, but who else acted deceitfully in this situation?

93. Was any of this Isaac's fault?

94. Was any of this Esau's fault?

95. The name Jacob means *he grasps the heel*, which was another way of saying *he deceives*. When Esau told Isaac that Jacob was named rightly, what did he mean?

96. What did Isaac tell Esau that the blessing on Jacob included?

97. When Esau repeated his request for a blessing from Isaac and then wept aloud, what did Isaac do?

—— **Read Genesis 27:41-46**

98. How did Esau feel about Jacob since the blessing incident?

99. What did he plan to do for his revenge?

100. What did Rebekah do when she heard about Esau's plan?

101. What did she say she would do once Esau had calmed down?

102. What was her reasoning behind this action?

103. What excuse did Rebekah give Isaac for Jacob's quick departure?

Rebekah

104. Re-read Genesis 26:34. What kind of women had Esau married?

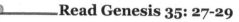 **Read Genesis 35: 27-29**

105. How long did Isaac live?

106. Who buried Isaac?

107. Do these verses say how long Rebekah lived?

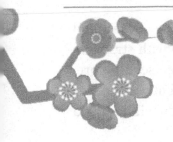

Short Essay Questions

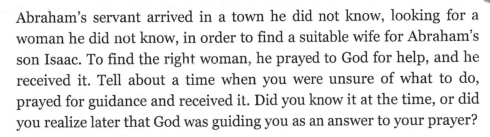

1. Abraham's servant arrived in a town he did not know, looking for a woman he did not know, in order to find a suitable wife for Abraham's son Isaac. To find the right woman, he prayed to God for help, and he received it. Tell about a time when you were unsure of what to do, prayed for guidance and received it. Did you know it at the time, or did you realize later that God was guiding you as an answer to your prayer?

Rebekah

 2. Imagine you're Rebekah. One day you're doing your chores, and the next you're leaving your family and home to go with strangers to another country to marry a cousin you've never seen before. There are no planes, trains or cars, so it's possible that you'll never see your family again. How do you feel? Why are you willing to do such a thing? Re-read Genesis 24 for ideas.

 3. God used Rebekah to comfort Isaac as he grieved the death of his mother Sarah. Can you think of a time when God used you to comfort someone? Write about that time. If you cannot think of such a time, what could you do to comfort someone in the future? What talents has God given you that can be used to comfort others, particularly those who grieve the death of a loved one?

4. According to Genesis 25:28, Isaac loved Esau and Rebekah loved Jacob. Was this favoritism the only reason Rebekah wanted to deceive her husband and secure the blessing for Jacob? Or was there another reason? Re-read Genesis 25:23, noting that in the last line, it says that the Lord told Rebekah, "....and the elder shall serve the younger." Compare that to Genesis 27:40. Make a case for whether or not Rebekah was trying to make God's promise come true.

Rebekah

5. The fact that Isaac and Rebekah played favorites with their children resulted in difficult family relationships. If you're someday blessed with children of your own, what are some ways that you and your husband could foster healthy relationships with each of your children?

6. The blessing Isaac gave "Esau" (Jacob) in Genesis 27:27-29 would impact not just Jacob but also his descendants, who would be Isaac and Rebekah's descendants, too. Compare the good things mentioned in that blessing to those promised to Abraham by God in Genesis 12:2-3. What are the similarities between the two blessings?

Discussion Starters for Mothers and Daughters

❀ Rebekah married into a family that had no older woman present. How can a mother or mother-in-law be a help to a new bride? How can she be a hindrance?

❀ Rebekah's twin sons were very different. Esau was born red and hairy, and eventually became a hunter, while Jacob had smooth skin and a quiet manner, and was not as adventuresome as his brother. Talk about members of your own family (both your immediate circle and your extended family), and find examples of siblings who are very different. What characteristics and abilities does each person bring to the family? Why do you think God sends parents such a variety of offspring?

❀ Jacob was favored by his mother Rebekah, while Isaac favored his and Rebekah's other son, Esau. What was the result of their favoritism? How

Rebekah

can parents make an effort not to favor one child over another?

 Esau married Hittite women, who were a source of grief to Esau's parents, Isaac and Rebekah, according to Genesis 26:35. One reason why these women grieved their husband's parents is that the Hittites were not worshippers of God. Find out what God said about the Hittites, and also about marriage to nonbelievers, in Deuteronomy 7:1-4. Then read 2 Corinthians 6:14-16 and discuss what God requires of the Christian's choice of a spouse.

 In Genesis 25:22, we learn that Rebekah's babies "jostled each other within her." This must have been pretty intense jostling, enough to make her ask God why it was happening. Pregnancy can be scary at times, especially when the new mother doesn't know what to expect as her body changes. Discuss how a woman who is expecting a child can rely on God for comfort and peace. Share with your daughter any Bible verses that helped you when you were awaiting her arrival, whether you gave birth to her or adopted her.

Notes:

Rachel and Leah

Genesis 28 to 49
Time Period: 1966-1859 BC

Rachel and Leah were sisters who shared a husband. The rivalry between them would make their relationship difficult, but the sons they bore him would someday become the twelve tribes of Israel.

 Read Genesis 28:1-5, then answer the following questions:

1. What place did Isaac tell Jacob to visit in his search for a wife?

2. Whose house was Jacob supposed to visit?

3.   What was he supposed to do there?

4.   What did Isaac do for Jacob before Jacob left to find a wife?

5.   Did Jacob go to the place Isaac told him to go to?

Read Genesis 29:1-14

6.   As Jacob approached the land his father had sent him to, what did he see?

7.   What did he ask the shepherds he encountered there?

8.   What was the second question he asked them?

9.   What was their answer?

10. Why was this important to Jacob?

11. What else did the shepherds tell him?

12. What was Rachel's job?

Rachel and Leah

13. How did Jacob help Rachel?

14. What did Jacob do after he helped Rachel?

15. How did Rachel react?

16. How was Laban related to Jacob?

17. How did Laban greet Jacob?

Read Genesis 29:15-21

18. What did Laban ask Jacob?

19. Describe Laban's daughters.

20. For what wages did Jacob say he would work for Laban?

21. Why did Jacob choose those wages?

22. Did Laban agree to those wages?

23. How many years did Jacob work to "earn" Rachel?

24. How did the time pass for Jacob?

25. After the time was up, did Laban offer the wages, or did Jacob have to ask for them?

Read Genesis 29:22-30

26. What did Laban do to fulfill his promise of Jacob's wages?

27. What did Laban do that did *not* fulfill his promise of Jacob's wages?

28. How did Jacob feel about Laban's behavior?

29. What was Laban's excuse?

30. What did Laban suggest to Jacob so he could have what he wanted?

31. Did Jacob follow through on Laban's suggestion?

32. How did Jacob feel about Leah and Rachel?

Rachel and Leah

 **Read Genesis 29:31-35**

33. What did God do for Leah when He saw that she was not loved?

34. What was Rachel's situation at this time?

35. What did God send Leah?

36. Why did Leah think God had sent her a child?

37. What did Leah think would happen because of Reuben's birth?

38. What happened after Reuben was born?

39. Why did Leah say this latest event had occurred?

40. What happened after the second son was born?

41. What did Leah think would happen after the third son was born?

42. What happened after Levi's birth?

43. What did Leah say would happen after this?

44. What happened after Judah's birth?

Read Genesis 30:1-8

45. How many children did Leah have so far?

46. How many children did Rachel have so far?

47. How did Rachel feel about this?

48. To whom did she express her feelings about this?

49. What was that person's response?

50. How did Rachel decide to solve her problem?

51. What was the result of Rachel's solution?

52. What was Rachel's reaction to this event?

Rachel and Leah

53. What happened next, in verse 7?

54. What was Rachel's reaction this time?

Read Genesis 30:9-13

55. What did Leah do when she saw that she had stopped having children?

56. What was the result of this action?

57. What was Leah's reaction to this?

58. What happened next, in verse 12?

59. How did Leah react this time?

Read Genesis 30:14-24

60. At this time in history, many people believed that the root of the mandrake plant would help a woman conceive a child. In verse 14, who brought Leah some mandrake plants?

61. What did Rachel then ask Leah to do?

62. How did Leah respond to Rachel's request?

63. What did Rachel then offer to Leah to make her do what she wanted?

64. Did Leah agree to Rachel's offer?

65. What did Leah tell Jacob?

66. What was the result of this event, and why, according to the Bible, did it happen?

67. Whom did Leah credit with this event?

68. When Rachel first made her request of Leah, did she intend the end result to be another child for Leah?

69. Leah named the child Issachar, which means *reward*. What happened after she had Issachar, according to verse 19?

70. To whom did she give credit for this event?

Rachel and Leah

71. What did Leah hope this would do to Jacob?

72. What happened to Leah in verse 21?

73. At this point in the story, how many children did Leah and Rachel each have?

74. What did God do for Rachel in verse 22?

75. What happened to Rachel then?

76. What was Rachel's response to this?

In the remainder of Genesis 30, Jacob tried to take his large and growing family back to Canaan, but had to work out his wages with Laban first. Laban attempted to cheat Jacob, then left the area. But God allowed Jacob to prosper anyway. At the beginning of Genesis 31, God told Jacob to go back to his homeland, and that He would be with Jacob and his family.

Read Genesis 31:14-21

77. How did Rachel and Leah feel about leaving their father for Jacob's homeland?

78. Whom and what did Jacob take to Canaan?

79. What had Rachel done while her father was shearing his sheep?

80. How did Jacob deceive Laban?

Read Genesis 31:22-37

81. What did Laban do when he found out Jacob had run away?

82. What happened in the hill country of Gilead?

83. Who came to Laban in a dream and told him how to deal with Jacob?

84. What questions did Laban ask Jacob once he saw him?

85. Why did Jacob say he ran away?

86. What did he say about the disappearance of Laban's household gods?

87. According to verse 32, of what was Jacob unaware?

88. Did Laban find the gods in Leah's tent?

Rachel and Leah

89. Did Laban find the gods in the tent of the two maidservants?

90. Did Laban find the gods in Rachel's tent?

91. Where were the gods?

92. How did Jacob react when Laban couldn't find the gods?

In the rest of Genesis 31, Jacob aired his complaints about how Laban treated him, and told how God had protected him. Laban expressed his desire to keep his daughters and grandchildren near him and suggested they make a covenant between them. They agreed that Jacob would not harm Laban's daughters and grandchildren, and that Laban and Jacob would not harm each other. Then Laban kissed and blessed his daughters and grandchildren, and returned home.

In Genesis 32, as Jacob and his family headed back toward his homeland, he prepared to meet his brother Esau, but with caution, as they had parted on bad terms. Jacob sent many gifts ahead to Esau. One night Jacob wrestled with a man who wrenched Jacob's hip because Jacob wouldn't let him go. Jacob requested a blessing, and the man told him his name would be changed from Jacob to Israel. Later, Jacob realized the man was God.

Read Genesis 33:1-11

93. When Jacob looked up and saw Esau approaching, who did he see with Esau?

94. What did Jacob do then?

95. In what order did Jacob arrange himself and his family?

> Front row:

> Second row:

> Third row:

> Back row:

96. How did Esau react to seeing Jacob?

97. How did Jacob identify his family members?

98. What did Jacob's family members do when they met Esau?

99. What did Esau say about the gifts Jacob brought him?

100. How did Jacob respond?

101. What did Esau do then?

Rachel and Leah

Read Genesis 35:16-20

102. What happened to Rachel when they were some distance from Ephrath?

103. What did the midwife tell Rachel?

104. What was Rachel's last act?

105. What did Jacob name the baby?

106. What happened to Rachel?

107. What did Jacob do for Rachel?

 Read Genesis 48:7

108. How did Jacob feel about Rachel's death?

 Read Genesis 49:29-31

109. Where was Leah buried, and with whom?

Short Essay Questions

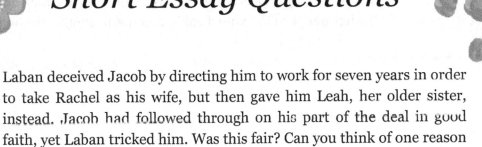

1. Laban deceived Jacob by directing him to work for seven years in order to take Rachel as his wife, but then gave him Leah, her older sister, instead. Jacob had followed through on his part of the deal in good faith, yet Laban tricked him. Was this fair? Can you think of one reason why God might have allowed Jacob to experience being on the receiving end of a deception? (Clue: Genesis 27:36)

2. Poor Leah! She woke up the morning after her wedding to find that her husband was disappointed that she wasn't her younger (and prettier) sister Rachel. Then, a week later, he also married Rachel. How do you think she felt? As the years went by, in whom did she find comfort? (See Genesis 29:32, 33, 35 and Genesis 30:18 and 20).

Rachel and Leah

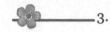 3. In the times in which Jacob, Leah and Rachel lived, being given children was considered a blessing from God, and being barren was considered a curse from Him, and therefore a disgrace. Use this knowledge to describe the relationship between the sisters Rachel and Leah. (Note Leah's comment about "the women" in Genesis 30:13.)

 4. While the Bible notes in several places that Jacob loved Rachel, there are no specific references describing how Rachel felt about Jacob. Use the following verses to help you in determining whether or not Rachel loved Jacob, and also to get some idea of Rachel's character: Genesis 30:1, 8, 15, and 24, and Genesis 31:19 and 34-35. Use the information you find to write a paragraph about what Rachel was like.

5. Jacob's sons would become very important to the future of Israel. Re-read Genesis 29:31 to 30:24, and also Genesis 35:16-18, recording the births of Jacob's sons in order. Note who was born to which mother. Then fill out the following chart:

Birth Order	Name	Birth Mother
1		
2		
3		
4		
5		
6		
7		
8		
9		
10		
11		
12		

Rachel and Leah

6. Jacob was married to both Rachel and Leah; being married to more than one person at a time is called *polygamy*. Look up and read the following verses: Leviticus 18:18, Deuteronomy 17:17, 1 Timothy 3:2 and 3:12, and Titus 1:6. In light of those verses, read Genesis 2:18 and 2:24. Then use any or all of these verses to defend what you believe God says about polygamy.

7. In Genesis 30:6, barren Rachel gave her maidservant Bilhah to Jacob in hopes that they would produce a child. When that did happen, Rachel said God had vindicated her. Then Leah, who had stopped having children, gave her maidservant Zilpah to Jacob in hopes that *they* would produce a child. That did happen, then later, in Genesis 30:18, when Leah gave birth to her own fifth son, she said, "God has rewarded me for giving my maidservant to my husband." Do you think Rachel and Leah were correct in their understanding of why God did what He did? Use God's definition of marriage to explain your answer.

Discussion Starters for Mothers and Daughters

🌸 Rachel and Leah shared the same husband. How would you feel about sharing your husband with another woman? What would be your reaction if she had many children and you did not? Would the fact that the other wife was your sister make the situation harder or easier?

🌸 God invented monogamy, not polygamy. Compare the two before discussing how God uses monogamy to protect women.

🌸 After a long spell of infertility, Rachel finally gave birth to a son. She named the baby Joseph, and then said, "May the Lord add to me another son." Her competition with her sister led her to be greedy instead of grateful. What should we do when our prayers seem to contain more requests than thanks?

Rachel and Leah

The Midwives, the Princess and Miriam

Exodus 1, 2 ,15 and Numbers 12
Time Period: 1526-1407 BC

Rachel's son Joseph grew up to become the right-hand man of the Pharaoh of Egypt. He was put in charge of the entire land of Egypt at the age of 30. Joseph's brothers eventually came to Egypt, where they and Joseph would stay while God fulfilled his promise to Joseph's grandfather Isaac: "I will bless you and will increase the number of your descendants for the sake of my servant Abraham." (Genesis 26:24)

Joseph's descendants were eventually taken as slaves in Egypt. God chose Moses to lead them out. God used midwives, a princess and Moses' sister Miriam to protect Moses so that he could eventually fulfill God's plan for His captive people.

Read Exodus 1:1-22, then answer the following questions:

1. According to verse 7, what happened to Joseph's descendants, the Israelites?

2. How did the new king feel about the Israelites?

3. What did the Egyptians do to the Israelites?

4. How did the Israelites react to this?

5. How did the Egyptians treat the Israelites as they increased in number?

6. What were the names of the Hebrew midwives?

7. What is a midwife? (Use a dictionary if you don't already know.)

8. What did the Egyptian king tell the midwives to do when they helped the Israelite women in childbirth?

9. Did the midwives follow the king's order?

The Midwives, the Princess and Miriam

10. Why or why not?

11. What did the king ask the midwives?

12. What was the midwives' response to the king (Pharaoh)?

13. How did God bless the midwives for their obedience to Him?

14. What did Pharaoh tell his people to do to the Israelites?

Read Exodus 2:1-10

15. Why did the Levite woman hide her baby? (Note: Levites were Israelites.)

16. How long did she hide him?

17. What did she do when she couldn't hide him any longer?

18. Who stood watch over him?

19. Who saw the basket in the reeds?

20. What did she do about the basket?

21. What was her reaction to the basket's contents?

22. Who offered to help the princess with the little bundle she had found?

23. What was the offer of help?

24. Did the princess accept the offer of help?

25. Who was brought to help?

26. Did the princess know who this "helper" really was?

27. What did the princess offer for this help?

28. What happened to the baby when he got older?

29. What did the princess name the baby?

The Midwives, the Princess and Miriam

Moses would grow up to become the person God chose to lead the Israelites out of slavery. Aided by his brother Aaron, Moses led the Israelites out of Egypt and across the Red Sea, which God parted for them and then closed back over the pursuing Egyptians. Once the Israelites were safe on the other shore, Moses and the Israelites praised God in song. At this point in the story we read about Moses' sister Miriam, the same sister who protected him when he was an infant hidden in the reeds on the shore of the Nile River.

Read Exodus 15:19-21

30. How is Miriam described in verse 20?

31. What is a prophetess? (Use the dictionary if you need it.)

32. Look up Numbers 26:59; what were the names of Miriam's family members?

33. How did Miriam praise God for delivering the Israelites from the Egyptians?

34. What did the women among the Israelites do?

35. What did Miriam say about God?

36. Read Micah 6:4; was Miriam one of the leaders of the Israelites?

Read Numbers 12:1-16

37. What did Miriam and Aaron begin to do to Moses?

38. What did they ask about Moses?

39. Who heard them talking about Moses?

40. What kind of man was Moses?

41. What did God do in verse 4?

42. When did He do this?

43. How did God arrive?

44. Whom did He call by name?

45. How did they respond?

46. What two things did God say He does for prophets?

The Midwives, the Princess and Miriam

47. Did he do these things for Moses?

48. What adjective did God use to describe Moses in verse 7?

49. How did God describe his relationship with Moses?

50. What question did God ask Miriam and Aaron?

51. How did God feel about them?

52. After God left their presence, and the cloud lifted from the tabernacle, what did they see?

53. Using a dictionary for help, describe Miriam's condition.

54. After he saw what happened to Miriam, was Aaron repentant?

55. What did Aaron ask of Moses?

56. How did Moses respond to Aaron's request?

57. What happened to Miriam?

Short Essay Questions

1. Midwives Shiphrah and Puah disobeyed the king because they feared God. Even when Pharaoh questioned them directly about their actions, they did not back down, but instead misled him. Imagine you are Shiphrah or Puah, and write a paragraph or two describing your feelings after being ordered by Pharaoh to kill the Hebrew baby boys. Remember, you're an Israelite, and therefore a slave, so you have no rights in Egypt.

2. Before Moses' mother hid him in the reeds, he had been kept protected in his family's home. By disobeying the murderous edict of the Pharaoh, Moses' parents risked punishment by the Egyptians. Why did they take such a risk? Read Hebrews 11:23, then explain why Moses' parents hid him, and what gave them the courage to do so.

3. Miriam watched over her baby brother when he was lying among the reeds in a basket. She had to think fast when he was found, and reacted by offering to find a Hebrew woman to nurse the baby for the princess who had found him. Miriam's quick thinking resulted in her mother becoming the baby's paid caregiver, thus allowing the family to remain together. God used Miriam to protect her brother, even though she was not yet an adult (Exodus 2:8 refers to her as a girl). Looking back on your life so far, can you think of one or more times when God used you for His purposes? Describe what happened. How can you be open to God's leading in the future?

The Midwives, the Princess and Miriam

4. The book of Exodus does not indicate how Moses' mother (identified elsewhere in the book as Jochebed) felt about having to hide her baby in the reeds to save his life, but we can imagine how painful it must have been for her to leave him there. We can also imagine her joy when God allowed her to become the baby's nurse; the princess even let her take the baby home to care for him. Can you think of a time in your life, or in the life of your family, that God turned something negative into a blessing? Describe what happened, and what it taught you about God.

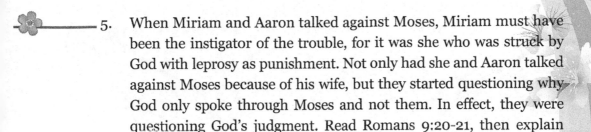

5. When Miriam and Aaron talked against Moses, Miriam must have been the instigator of the trouble, for it was she who was struck by God with leprosy as punishment. Not only had she and Aaron talked against Moses because of his wife, but they started questioning why God only spoke through Moses and not them. In effect, they were questioning God's judgment. Read Romans 9:20-21, then explain why we have no right to question God's judgment.

6. God sent Miriam to help Moses lead the Israelites, according to Micah 6:4, yet He was very quick to discipline her when she acted dishonorably. Why did He punish her? Should she have felt rejected by God because He punished her? Are you being rejected by your parents when they punish you? Read Hebrews 12:5-6 before you answer.

The Midwives, the Princess and Miriam

Discussion Starters for Mothers and Daughters

Miriam and Aaron talked against Moses because of his Cushite wife. We know that Cush was another name for Ethiopia, and that Ethiopians had dark skin then (Jeremiah 13:23) as they do today. Therefore Moses' wife was likely dark-skinned. Some Bible scholars believe Miriam and Aaron criticized her because she was of another race, and that God's choice of punishment (leprosy, causing diseased skin that was "like snow," according to Numbers 12:10) was intended to make a statement about judging people by the color of their skin and viewing lighter skin as somehow better than dark skin. What does God think about judging people by the color of their skin? Look up and discuss 1 Samuel 16:7 and Galatians 2:6.

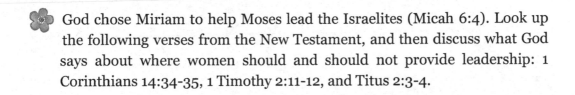

God chose Miriam to help Moses lead the Israelites (Micah 6:4). Look up the following verses from the New Testament, and then discuss what God says about where women should and should not provide leadership: 1 Corinthians 14:34-35, 1 Timothy 2:11-12, and Titus 2:3-4.

God had a very important job planned for Moses; He used women (the midwives, Jochebed, Miriam and the Egyptian princess) to protect and preserve him for that job. Discuss how God can use present-day mothers to protect and preserve their children for His purposes. Also, how can God use women who are *not* mothers to protect His children?

As midwives, Shiphrah and Puah helped women deliver their babies, which gave them immediate access to newborns. Yet they disobeyed the direct command of Pharaoh to kill the Hebrew boy babies and instead honored God with their work by allowing the babies to live. Think of the different careers available to women in the 21st century. How can a person honor God in each of them? Do either of you feel God calling you to a specific vocation? If so, in what ways could you honor God with that work?

Notes:

The Midwives, the Princess and Miriam

Rahab

Joshua 2 and 6:15-25
Time Period: 1406 BC

After Moses led the Israelites through the desert for 40 years, he died and was succeeded by Joshua, a man appointed by God to lead the Israelites into Canaan, the Promised Land. In taking over Canaan, Joshua's first assignment was to conquer the city of Jericho.

 Read Joshua 2:1-7, then answer the following questions:

1. Whom did Joshua send to check out Jericho?

2. Where did they go when they got to Jericho?

3. What is a prostitute? (Use your dictionary.)

4. Who was told that the Israelites were spying on Jericho?

5. To whom did he send a message about the spies?

6. What did he say in the message?

7. According to verse 4, what had Rahab done with the spies?

8. How did Rahab respond to the message?

9. Did Rahab tell the truth?

10. Where were the spies?

11. What did the king's men do?

12. Read Hebrews 11:31; why did Rahab hide the spies Joshua sent to Jericho?

Rahab

Read Joshua 2:8-14

13. What did Rahab tell the spies that night about their mission?

14. According to Rahab, how did the people of Jericho feel about the Israelites?

15. Why did the people of Jericho feel that way?

16. What favor did Rahab ask of the spies?

17. How did the spies respond to her request?

 Read Joshua 2:15-24

18. What did Rahab do for the spies?

19. What directions did she give them?

20. What did the spies tell Rahab to do as her part of their agreement?

21. What would happen to those who left her house once the Israelites attacked Jericho?

22. Who would take the blame if someone was hurt inside Rahab's house during the attack?

23. What would happen if Rahab told anyone what the spies were planning?

24. Did Rahab agree with what the spies told her?

25. What was the first thing Rahab did after the spies left her house?

26. Were the spies found by the king's men?

27. What good news did Joshua receive?

Led by Joshua, the Israelites crossed the Jordan River and prepared to attack the city of Jericho, which was tightly closed up with city gates locked, in anticipation of the attack. Joshua and the Israelites followed God's instructions and marched around the city once a day for six days. Then, on the seventh day, God brought down the wall of Jericho, and the Israelites attacked the city.

Read Joshua 6:15-25

28. When Joshua gave his people instructions for attacking the city of Jericho, which city residents did he say would be spared?

Rahab

29. What reason did he give for protecting those specific citizens of Jericho?

30. Once the city wall fell and the Israelites got inside, what did they do to those living in Jericho?

31. Where did Joshua send the spies?

32. Where did the spies take them?

33. What happened to the city of Jericho?

34. According to verse 25, what happened to Rahab?

Read Matthew 1:5

35. Whom would Rahab eventually marry?

36. What was the name of their son?

37. Who would be the most important person in Rahab's family line someday? See Matthew 1:16 if you need help.

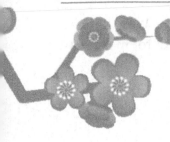

Short Essay Questions

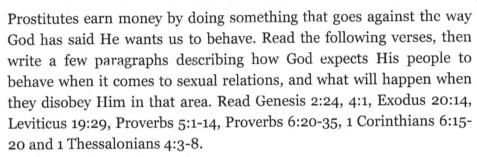

1. Prostitutes earn money by doing something that goes against the way God has said He wants us to behave. Read the following verses, then write a few paragraphs describing how God expects His people to behave when it comes to sexual relations, and what will happen when they disobey Him in that area. Read Genesis 2:24, 4:1, Exodus 20:14, Leviticus 19:29, Proverbs 5:1-14, Proverbs 6:20-35, 1 Corinthians 6:15-20 and 1 Thessalonians 4:3-8.

Rahab

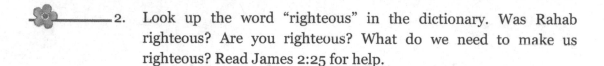

2. Look up the word "righteous" in the dictionary. Was Rahab righteous? Are you righteous? What do we need to make us righteous? Read James 2:25 for help.

3. Even though Rahab was a prostitute, God used her to help the Israelites take over the city of Jericho. We are all sinners, and yet God uses us for His purposes. Write about a time when God used you, a sinner, for His purpose.

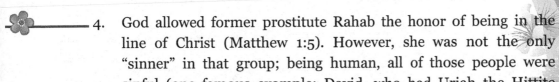

4. God allowed former prostitute Rahab the honor of being in the line of Christ (Matthew 1:5). However, she was not the only "sinner" in that group; being human, all of those people were sinful (one famous example: David, who had Uriah the Hittite killed so that he could marry Uriah's wife Bathsheba). How does this knowledge make you feel? Before you answer, consider how Paul felt about it; read 1 Timothy 1:12-17.

Rahab

Discussion Starters for Mothers and Daughters

The protection of women is one result of following God's rules for sexual behavior (review Bible verses listed in Short Essay Question #1). What kinds of things will we be protected from when we obey God in this area?

At different times and in various cultures, women have resorted to prostitution in order to support themselves and their children. Look up the following verses together: Matthew 6:31-33 and 10:29-31. How do these verses help us understand that we will *never* need to resort to sin in order to survive?

Notes:

Rahab

Deborah and Jael

Judges 4 to 5
Time Period: 1217 BC

Deborah, a judge, and Jael, a nomadic "tent-wife," were two very different women told about in the Bible, but we'll study them together because their stories intertwine.

 Read Judges 4:1-10, then answer the following questions:

1. What did God see regarding the Israelites' behavior at that time?

2. How did God respond to the Israelites' behavior?

3. Who was the commander of Jabin's army?

4. What was the commander like?

5. What did the Israelites say to God?

6. Who was leading Israel at that time?

7. Where was this leader to be found?

8. What did the leader usually do for the Israelites in that location?

9. For whom did Deborah send in response to the Israelites' complaint about Sisera?

10. What did she command him to do?

11. What did Deborah say she would do then?

12. How did Barak respond to Deborah's plans?

Deborah and Jael

13. What did Deborah say after hearing Barak's response to her request?

14. To whom did Deborah say God would give the honor of stopping Sisera?

15. Where did Deborah and Barak go then?

16. What did Barak do there?

17. How many men joined Deborah and Barak at Kedesh?

Read Judges 4:11-18

18. Where did Heber the Kenite pitch his tent?

19. What did Sisera do when he heard that Barak had gone up to Mount Tabor?

20. What instructions did Deborah give Barak?

21. Whom did she say had gone ahead of him and would give him a victory over Sisera?

22. Did Barak follow Deborah's instructions?

23. Did Barak's army win?

24. Read verse 15 carefully: who does the Bible say actually won the battle ("routed .... and all his army by the sword")?

25. What did the losing leader and his men do then?

26. What happened to the army that lost?

27. What happened to their leader?

28. Why did he go there?

29. What kind of greeting did he receive there?

Read Judges 4:19-24

30. What was the first thing he told Jael to do?

31. Did she do as he told her?

Deborah and Jael

32. What was the second thing he told Jael to do?

33. Did she do as he told her?

34. What did she do?

35. What happened to Sisera?

36. Who came near the tent?

37. What did Jael tell this person?

38. How did he learn Jael was telling the truth?

39. According to verse 23, who subdued Jabin that day?

40. What then happened to the Israelites?

41. What happened to Jabin?

Read Judges 5, the song of praise Deborah and Barak sang to God the day their enemy was destroyed, then list as many mentions as you can find about:

42. Deborah

43. Jael

44. God

45. According to Judges 5:31, what happened to the land in which the Israelites were living?

Deborah and Jael

Short Essay Questions

1. Go back through Judges 4-5 and note any descriptions you find that give you clues to what Deborah's life was like, then do the same for Jael. Do you think they lived similar lives or different lives? How did God use each one and her position in life to punish the oppressor of the Israelites? What does this tell you about the kind of people God uses to do his will?

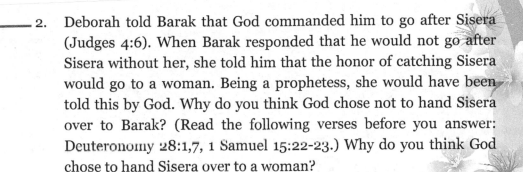

2. Deborah told Barak that God commanded him to go after Sisera (Judges 4:6). When Barak responded that he would not go after Sisera without her, she told him that the honor of catching Sisera would go to a woman. Being a prophetess, she would have been told this by God. Why do you think God chose not to hand Sisera over to Barak? (Read the following verses before you answer: Deuteronomy 28:1,7, 1 Samuel 15:22-23.) Why do you think God chose to hand Sisera over to a woman?

3. Women do not generally have as much upper-body strength as men, yet Jael was able to drive a tent peg through Sisera's temple. Even more surprisingly, Sisera did not wake up when this was happening. How can these events be explained? See Genesis 2:21 and the first part of Genesis 18:14 for help. How can this encourage you when you're faced with a task that seems impossible?

Deborah and Jael

Discussion Starters for Mothers and Daughters

We aren't told if Deborah was a working mother, but we do know she was a working wife (Judges 4:4). Using a concordance, look together for Bible verses that you believe indicate whether or not a wife should work outside the home. What if the wife is also a mother? Use the concordance to find Bible verses that you believe indicate whether or not mothers should work outside the home.

At the end of Deborah's song (Judges 5), verse 28 manages to convey in just a few sentences the concern of a mother over her son who is late coming home. Discuss together the fears a mother has when a child runs late or, worse, goes missing, and why children should let their parents know whenever they're running late or their plans have changed.

Notes:

Deborah and Jael

Ruth

Ruth 1 to 4
Time Period: 11th Century BC

The book of Ruth is a beautiful story of love within a family, and it offers women of all ages a wonderful role model in the person of Ruth.

 Read Ruth 1:1-18, then answer the following questions:

1. Why did the man and his family go to live in the country of Moab?

2. What were the names of the members of this family?

3. What happened to the father after the family moved to Moab?

4. The sons each married women from Moab; what were the names of their wives?

5. What happened after the family had lived in Moab for about ten years?

6. What news from Judah did the family receive?

7. Who is credited with providing food for the people of Judah?

8. What did Naomi decide to do after hearing the news?

9. Who was with Naomi when she started out on her journey?

10. What did Naomi tell her companions?

11. How did they react to her words?

12. What did Naomi say her reasons were for telling them what she did?

13. How did Naomi feel about God?

Ruth

14. Who kissed her mother-in-law good-bye first?

15. What did Naomi tell Ruth?

16. Did Ruth agree with Naomi? What did she tell Naomi?

17. What did Naomi decide, and why?

Read Ruth 1:19-22

18. What kind of reception awaited the women in Bethlehem?

19. What did Naomi tell the people of the town to call her, and why?

20. When the women arrived in Bethlehem, what time of year was it?

Read Ruth 2:1-9

21. What was the name of the relative Naomi had on her husband's side of the family?

22. What did Ruth ask Naomi for permission to do?

23. In whose field did Ruth end up?

24. Who arrived and greeted the harvesters in the field?

25. Did Boaz notice Ruth?

26. What did the foreman say about Ruth?

27. Once Boaz learned who Ruth was, what did he tell her?

28. What had Boaz done for Ruth's protection?

29. What did Boaz do for Ruth's comfort?

Read Ruth 2:10-17

30. What did Ruth ask Boaz?

31. What was Boaz' response?

32. What did Boaz do for Ruth at mealtime?

Ruth

33. What did Boaz order his men to do for Ruth?

34. How much barley did Ruth glean?

In the following section, Naomi refers to Boaz as one of their family's kinsman-redeemers. A kinsman-redeemer was a relative who was willing to help care for family members. In those days, a widow like Ruth would be expected to marry one of her husband's brothers so that they could have children and carry on her husband's family line. But Ruth's only brother-in-law had also died, so there was no brother for her to marry. Widows had to rely on family for their support, which explains Naomi's suggestion that they look to one of the family's kinsman-redeemers for help.

Read Ruth 2:18-23

35. What did Ruth do with the barley she had gleaned?

36. What did Naomi ask Ruth after she saw the barley?

37. When Ruth told Naomi that she had been working for Boaz, what did Naomi say about him?

38. Did Naomi want Ruth to continue to glean in Boaz' fields? What did she tell Ruth about that?

39. Did Ruth obey Naomi?

Read Ruth 3:1-6

40. What did Naomi think she should be doing for Ruth?

41. Who did she have in mind for Ruth?

42. What did she tell Ruth to do that night? (List all of her instructions.)

43. Did Ruth obey Naomi?

 Read Ruth 3:7-15

44. Where did Boaz lie down?

45. What did Ruth do then?

46. When did Boaz discover Ruth there?

47. How did Ruth identify herself?

48. What did Ruth suggest Boaz do?

Ruth

49. How did Boaz react to Ruth's suggestion?

50. Read verse 11 again. Did Boaz think Ruth's reputation would be tarnished by being on the threshing floor with him overnight?

51. Did Boaz become her kinsman-redeemer that night? Why or why not?

52. Did Ruth spend the night on the threshing floor?

53. When did Ruth leave the threshing floor?

54. What did Boaz do for her before she went home?

Read Ruth 3:16-18

55. Did Ruth tell Naomi what had happened on the threshing floor?

56. What was Boaz' parting comment to Ruth?

57. What did Naomi tell Ruth to do next?

58. Did Naomi think Boaz would do something about the situation?

Read Ruth 4:1-12

59. Where did Boaz go?

60. What word in verse 1 indicates when Boaz did this?

61. What did the kinsman-redeemer do when he saw Boaz?

62. Who else did Boaz invite to the meeting with the kinsman-redeemer?

63. What did Boaz suggest to the kinsman-redeemer?

64. Did the kinsman-redeemer agree to Boaz' suggestion?

65. What else did Boaz tell the kinsman-redeemer?

66. How did this additional information affect the kinsman-redeemer?

67. What was the kinsman-redeemer's reasoning for his decision?

68. What did the kinsman-redeemer do to finalize his decision?

Ruth

69. What did that action symbolize?

70. What did Boaz do after the kinsman-redeemer made his final decision?

71. What was Boaz' reasoning for this?

72. How did the town elders respond to Boaz?

73. Was Boaz fulfilling his role as kinsman-redeemer?

74. List the blessings requested for Boaz in verses 11 to 12.

Read Ruth 4:13-22

75. Who married Ruth?

76. What was the result of their union, and who made it happen?

77. What was the reaction of Naomi's friends to this news?

78. What did the women say would happen to Naomi?

79. What did the women say about Ruth?

80. What did Naomi do once the baby was born?

81. What did Boaz and Ruth name their baby?

82. Obed would eventually have a son and grandson who are very prominent in the Bible. What were their names?

83. List the family line of Boaz and Obed's ancestor Perez below.

84. Look up Matthew 1:5 and find the names of Boaz, Ruth and Obed; why are they listed there?

Ruth

Short Essay Questions

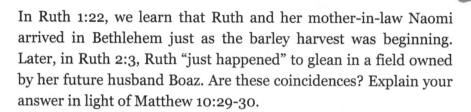

1. In Ruth 1:22, we learn that Ruth and her mother-in-law Naomi arrived in Bethlehem just as the barley harvest was beginning. Later, in Ruth 2:3, Ruth "just happened" to glean in a field owned by her future husband Boaz. Are these coincidences? Explain your answer in light of Matthew 10:29-30.

2. Ruth was a loving and unselfish person, and a wonderful role model for young women even today. Look up the following verses in the book of Ruth and explain how each illustrates Ruth's good qualities:

Ruth 1:16-17

Ruth 2:2-3

Ruth 2:13

Ruth 2:17

Ruth 2:22-23

Ruth 3:3-5

Ruth 3:10

Ruth

3. Write a few paragraphs about a time when someone was unselfish in caring for you. Then list a few ways you can act unselfishly towards your family and friends.

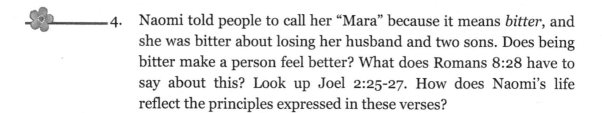

4. Naomi told people to call her "Mara" because it means *bitter*, and she was bitter about losing her husband and two sons. Does being bitter make a person feel better? What does Romans 8:28 have to say about this? Look up Joel 2:25-27. How does Naomi's life reflect the principles expressed in these verses?

5. There are many references to barley and wheat ("grain") in this book. Ruth gleaned barley and wheat, Naomi asked her how much grain she found, and Boaz provided Ruth with extra grain. The reason grain was so important is that it was all Ruth and Naomi had to eat because they were widows with no one to support them. Today, we have many, many food choices. While we live in such a wealthy society compared to the rest of the world, we often take the availability of food for granted. List some ways you can be more appreciative of the food available to you every day.

6. After the deaths of the men in their family, Naomi and Ruth were left utterly alone. In the society in which they lived, there were no jobs available for them to take so they could support themselves. They must have been frightened and worried, yet they did not give in to fear. Instead they returned to Bethlehem, where God used Boaz to help them. Do you ever feel helpless and worried? How can the example of Naomi and Ruth be encouraging to you? (Be specific.)

Ruth

Discussion Starters for Mothers and Daughters

Naomi showed her faith in God in several places in the book of Ruth by attributing both the good and the difficult events in life to Him. For example, in Ruth 1:9-10, rather than tell her daughters-in-law that she hoped they'd find new husbands, she told them that she hoped *the Lord* would find them new husbands. In Ruth 1:13 and 1:21, she shared her belief that her widowhood and the loss of her sons were due to the Lord's hand going out against her. Share with your daughter some examples of God's hand in your life.

Ruth found God through her relationship with Naomi, as evidenced by her words, "thy God (shall be) my God." How can you lead others to God through your relationships with them? Share with your daughter any stories you may have about someone you know (maybe even you?) who was led to Christ as a result of the influence of a friend or loved one.

Naomi gave Ruth some mystifying instructions: she told her to wash and perfume herself and dress in her best clothes before uncovering Boaz' feet while he was lying down on the threshing floor. Not being Hebrew, Ruth wouldn't have understood the reason for doing these things, yet she did them out of obedience to Naomi, trusting that there *was* a good reason. Does your daughter obey you even when she doesn't understand the reason for your request? Talk with her about the necessity of obedience to God, no matter what.

 After Ruth reported to Naomi that Boaz must first contact a man who was more closely related to their family before he could take on the role of her kinsman-redeemer, Naomi told Ruth to wait and see what happened. Describe to your daughter what has occurred when you've waited for God to work instead of trying to make things happen yourself.

Notes:

Ruth

Hannah

1 Samuel 1 to 2
Time Period: 1080-1010 BC

Hannah was a woman of faith who was rewarded for her trust and sacrifice. God used her faith to bring forth a judge and deliverer of His people.

 Read 1 Samuel 1:1-8, then answer the following questions:

1. What do we learn about Elkanah in verse 2?

2. Did Peninnah have children?

3. Did Hannah have children?

4. Why did Elkanah go to Shiloh each year?

5. What were the names of the priests?

6. What was the priests' father's name?

7. What did Elkanah always share with his family on the day of the sacrifice?

8. How did he divide it among his family members?

9. What two facts explain why Elkanah gave one of his family members a double portion of the meat?

10. Why did Peninnah tease Hannah?

11. How often did Peninnah do this to Hannah?

12. How did Hannah react to Peninnah's teasing?

13. What did Elkanah ask Hannah when she reacted to Peninnah's teasing?

Hannah

Read 1 Samuel 1:9-18

14. What did Hannah do when everyone had finished eating and drinking at Shiloh?

15. Who was sitting by the temple doorpost?

16. What did Hannah do then?

17. How is her mood described in verse 10?

18. What did Hannah promise God in her prayer?

19. Who was watching her at this time?

20. What did he see Hannah doing?

21. What did he decide had happened to Hannah?

22. What did he say to Hannah?

23. What did Hannah tell him about herself then?

24. How did he respond after she explained what she was doing?

25. What did Hannah do after he said that?

26. Was she still upset? How do you know?

———Read 1 Samuel 1:19-20

27. Where did Elkanah and Hannah go the next day?

28. What happened to Hannah after they got there?

29. What does the name "Samuel" mean?

———Read 1 Samuel 1:21-28

30. Where did Elkanah go?

31. Who did not go with Elkanah?

32. Why not?

Hannah

33. How did Elkanah feel about that?

34. Why did Hannah make that choice?

35. Where did Hannah take Samuel once he was weaned?

36. What did they take with them on the trip?

37. Why did they take those things with them?

38. To whom was Samuel brought?

39. What did Hannah tell Eli?

Read 1 Samuel 2:1-11

40. What was the mood of Hannah's prayer?

41. What did she say about barren women in her prayer?

42. Where did she refer to God as the creator of life?

43. Did Samuel go home with Elkanah and Hannah?

Read 1 Samuel 2:18-21

44. What was little Samuel doing in Shiloh?

45. What did Samuel wear?

46. Who provided him with clothing?

47. What did Eli the priest do for Elkanah and Hannah when they came to Shiloh?

48. What did God do for Hannah?

To find out what became of Samuel, the little boy who was dedicated to God by his mother Hannah, read the following verses, then put them into your own words:

49. 1 Samuel 2:26

50. 1 Samuel 3:19 to 4:1

Hannah

51. 1 Samuel 7:6

52. 1 Samuel 7:15

53. 1 Samuel 25:1

54. Psalm 99:6

55. Hebrews 11:32-34

Short Essay Questions

1. Peninnah liked to torment Hannah by teasing her about her inability to have children. Peninnah herself had more than one son and daughter (1 Samuel 1:4). What kind of person do you think Peninnah was? Did she have a good reason for doing this? Read the following verses, then summarize what the Bible says about this subject: Psalm 15:1-3, Proverbs 25:23, James 1:26 and 3:5-6, and 1 Peter 3:10.

2. After Hannah prayed to God for a son, she stopped crying, and even began to eat again. What changed her mood? How do these verses apply to Hannah's situation, and to yours when you ask God for help? (Psalm 33:20, 37:4, 121:1-2, 145:13-16, Luke 17:6 and John 14:1)

3. Put yourself in Hannah's place: imagine giving up the small child God gave you because you had promised God you would do so. If you have younger siblings or cousins, try to imagine how you would feel if one of them, at around three years of age, was sent away, and you only saw him or her once a year after that. This should give you just a little taste of the depth of Hannah's sacrifice. Why did Hannah do such a thing? What does it say about her faith in God, and her relationship with Him?

4. Now that you've read about Samuel's accomplishments, would you say that Hannah's sacrifice bore fruit? Do you think Samuel would have become a great leader of Israel if he had not been dedicated to God from childhood by his mother Hannah, or could God have used him anyway?

Hannah

Discussion Starters for Mothers and Daughters

Although they may not reach the level of sacrifice Hannah did, most mothers make sacrifices for their children. Discuss with your daughter the sacrifices you've made as a mother, those your own mother made, and those made by others in your family history.

Hannah's burden was lifted after she presented her heartbreak and her request to God. In your life, when have you handed a burden over to God in prayer and felt relief? Use your experiences to discuss with your daughter how she can turn over *her* heartbreaks to God and find that same relief.

Notes:

Hannah

Abigail

1 Samuel 25
Time Period: 1010 BC

The story of Abigail is also a story from the life of David, the shepherd boy from Bethlehem who was anointed by Samuel, defeated the giant Goliath, and eventually became king. Abigail's wisdom saved the lives of others as well as her own. She humbled herself, yet ended up as royalty.

 Read 1 Samuel 25:1-3, then answer the following questions:

1. Where did David move to in verse 1?

2. Describe the wealthy man who lived there.

3. Describe the wealthy man's wife.

Read 1 Samuel 25:4-12

4. What did David hear about Nabal while he was in the desert?

5. Whom did David send to visit Nabal? Why?

6. How were David's messengers received?

7. What did David's messengers do?

Read 1 Samuel 25:13-17

8. How did David react to Nabal's response?

9. Read 1 Samuel 21:11; what was David's reputation?

10. Judging from what you've read so far, where was David going?

11. How many men went with David?

Abigail

12. How many men stayed behind?

13. Why didn't *all* of the men go with David?

14. In verses 14-17, a servant informs Nabal's wife Abigail of what's been going on. What did the servant say occurred when David sent his men to greet Nabal?

15. According to the servant, how had David's men treated Nabal's servants when they were out shearing the sheep in the desert?

16. Why did the servant say disaster was hanging over Nabal and his household?

17. Why didn't the servant warn Nabal of the impending danger?

Read 1 Samuel 25:18-22

18. What phrase indicates how quickly Abigail reacted to the servant's news?

19. What did Abigail pack up?

20. Where was she going with these items?

21. Who was going with her?

22. Did her husband know what she was up to?

23. Whom did Abigail meet in the ravine?

24. What was their intention?

Read 1 Samuel 25:23-31

25. What did Abigail do when she saw David?

26. What did she do after that?

27. Whom did she blame for the way David's men had been treated?

28. How did she describe her husband Nabal?

29. What did she say about David's men in verse 25?

Abigail

30. Whom did she say kept David from harming her family and household in retaliation for how David's men were treated?

31. To whom was she giving the gift, and with whom was it to be shared?

32. What did Abigail do in verses 28 to 29, and why did she do it?

33. In verses 30-31, what was Abigail suggesting to David?

34. What did Abigail ask of David for herself?

Read 1 Samuel 25:32-35

35. Whom did David credit with sending Abigail to meet him?

36. For what two reasons did David say Abigail should be blessed?

37. What did David say would have happened if Abigail had *not* come quickly to meet David and his men?

38. Did David accept Abigail's gift?

39. What did David tell Abigail to do?

40. What did he say about the things she had said?

Read 1 Samuel 25:36-42

41. What was Nabal doing when Abigail got home?

42. What kind of mood was Nabal in?

43. What did she say to him then?

44. What did she say to him the next morning?

45. How did Nabal react to Abigail's words?

46. Did God heal Nabal?

47. What did God do ten days later?

48. When David heard the news, who did he say caused Nabal's demise?

Abigail

49. Why did he say it happened?

50. What did David give credit to God for in David's own life?

51. What did David then ask Abigail to do?

52. How did he ask her?

53. Did Abigail agree to David's request?

54. Where did Abigail go?

55. Did she go alone?

What do you learn about Abigail in the following verses?

56. 1 Samuel 27:1-3

57. 1 Samuel 30: 1-5, 18

58. 2 Samuel 2:1-2

59. 2 Samuel 3:3

Abigail

Short Essay Questions

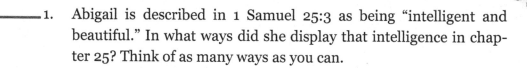

1. Abigail is described in 1 Samuel 25:3 as being "intelligent and beautiful." In what ways did she display that intelligence in chapter 25? Think of as many ways as you can.

2. When Abigail encountered David and his men in the ravine while on her way to bring them food, she told David that she would take the blame for how badly his men were treated by Nabal. Later, in verse 25, she told him she did not see David's men when they were insulted. These two statements of Abigail's may seem contradictory, but what she was doing was making clear to David that she would take responsibility for something she didn't do in order to prevent her family and household from being killed by his men. Describe a time when you, someone you know or someone you've read about (including fictional characters) was willing to take the blame for something they didn't do in order to protect others, and compare the incident to Abigail's situation.

Abigail

3. One of Abigail's great gifts was the gift of humility. Go back over the story of Abigail in the Bible and find and list examples of her humble attitude.

Now look up the following verses and write in your own words what God has to say about humility:

Deuteronomy 8:2-3

2 Chronicles 7:14

Proverbs 29:23

Matthew 18:1-4

Matthew 23:12

Philippians 2:4-11

James 4:6

James 4:10

1 Peter 5:5-6

Abigail

Discussion Starters for Mothers and Daughters

When Abigail learned from a servant about David's plan to take revenge on Nabal, she reacted quickly by packing up an enormous amount of food for David's soldiers. That she had so much food available and was able to have it packed up so quickly shows that she had an organized household. What situations in our daily family life require a prepared household? How can a mother make sure her family is prepared for emergencies?

When Nabal died, Abigail could have become wealthy and important in her own right, yet she chose to marry David instead. In this case, bypassing wealth and fame to become David's helper led Abigail on the path to becoming a wife and counselor of the king of Israel. In today's society, women often face similar decisions of whether to seek money and position on their own, or to live the "old-fashioned" way as a wife and mother. Discuss with your daughter how you've faced such decisions in your life; talk with her about how society views the role of a wife, and how God sees it, as evidenced in the Bible.

Abigail wisely talked David out of acting on his anger, thus preventing him from doing something he would regret. A mother must also do this with her children (and sometimes her husband). Think about times when your daughter has reacted with anger to something; how could you, your husband or others in your family help her to stop and think before reacting? Share with her ways that you've learned to keep yourself from reacting in anger.

Notes:

Abigail

Bathsheba

2 Samuel 11-12, 1 Chronicles 3 and 1 Kings 1-2
Time Period: 1002-970 BC

Like Abigail, Bathsheba became one of David's wives. Unlike Abigail, Bathsheba had an adulterous relationship with David before they were married. This story includes many lessons for us.

 Read 2 Samuel 3:2-5, then answer the following questions:

1. What were the names of David's wives thus far?

2. David's first wife (King Saul's daughter) is not mentioned in that list; read 1 Samuel 19:11 to find out her name.

3.   Read 2 Samuel 5:13; what did David do after he left Hebron?

4.   Did this behavior please God? (Read Deuteronomy 17:17 for help.)

Read 2 Samuel 11:1-5

5.   What phrase describes spring in this passage?

6.   Did King David go to war?

7.   What did the king do instead?

8.   What did the army do that spring?

9.   Where was David at this time?

10. What did he do one night when he couldn't sleep?

11. Whom did he see?

12. What was David's first reaction?

Bathsheba

13. What did David find out?

14. What was David's second reaction?

15. What happened at the first meeting of David and Bathsheba?

16. What message did Bathsheba soon send to David?

Read 2 Samuel 11:6-13

17. After receiving Bathsheba's news, what did David do?

18. Who then came to see David?

19. What did David order his visitor to do?

20. What did David send to him after he left?

21. Did Uriah do as David commanded him?

22. What did David later ask Uriah?

23. What was Uriah's response to David?

24. What did David invite Uriah to do after that?

25. What did David then do to Uriah?

26. Did Uriah go home after that?

Read 2 Samuel 11:14-25

27. Where did David decide to send Uriah?

28. David also sent a note for Joab with Uriah; what did it say?

29. Did Joab follow David's instructions?

30. What happened to Uriah?

31. Joab sent a message about Uriah to David; judging from verses 19-21, how did Joab expect David to react?

32. What did Joab tell the messenger to say last to David?

Bathsheba

33. What was David's reaction to the message?

34. Did David get angry at the message or messenger?

Read 2 Samuel 11:26-27

35. How is Bathsheba referred to in verse 26?

36. What was Bathsheba's reaction to the news David had received?

37. Where did Bathsheba go after the period of mourning was over?

38. What then happened between Bathsheba and David?

39. How did God feel about what had occurred?

Read 2 Samuel 12:1 and 7-14

40. Whom did God send to David?

41. What words in the message sent by God show clearly that He knew what David had done?

42. What did the messenger say would happen to David's family because of his behavior?

43. What was David's reaction to this?

44. What good thing did Nathan say God had already done for David?

45. What did Nathan say would happen to the child Bathsheba carried, because of David's sinful behavior?

Read 2 Samuel 12:15-24

46. In verse 15, what happened to David and Bathsheba's child?

47. How did this happen?

48. How did David react to this?

49. What happened to the child after a week had passed?

50. Why were David's servants afraid to tell him what had happened?

Bathsheba

51. How did David react to the news?

52. Why did David react this way?

53. The Bible clearly details David's reaction to this sad event, but does not refer to Bathsheba's reaction, except for one little clue. In which verse is Bathsheba's reaction suggested?

54. What did God then do for Bathsheba and David?

Read 1 Chronicles 3:5

55. How many times did God bless Bathsheba with children after she married David?

56. What were the names of her children?

Years later, when David was old and sickly, Adonijah (his son by one of his other wives) decided he wanted to be king, so he claimed himself as such without his father's knowledge or permission. However, God intended that David and Bathsheba's son Solomon would be king, and his parents had always known this. As He did when David sinned with Bathsheba, God sent Nathan the prophet to help remedy the situation.

Read 1 Kings 1:11-27

57. What news did Nathan bring Bathsheba?

58. What action did Nathan suggest that Bathsheba take?

59. How would Nathan back up Bathsheba?

60. What did Bathsheba tell David?

61. What fear did she express to him?

62. Did Nathan do for Bathsheba as he had promised?

63. How did Nathan end his visit?

Read 1 Kings 1:28-35

64. For whom did King David then call?

65. What did he tell that person?

66. How did that person react to the king's announcement?

67. What did David then order Zadok the priest and Nathan the prophet to do?

Bathsheba

Read 1 Kings 1:39-53

68. Did Zadok and Nathan do as David had commanded?

69. How did Adonijah react to the news of the new king of Israel?

70. Did Solomon punish Adonijah for trying to take his place on the throne?

Read 1 Kings 2:10-20

71. How long had David been king when he died?

72. How does the Bible describe the reign of the subsequent king, David's son Solomon?

73. What request did Adonijah bring to Bathsheba?

74. Why did he say he was bringing his request to her?

75. Did Bathsheba agree to go to King Solomon with his request?

76. How did King Solomon react when his mother came to see him?

77. How did he respond when she said she had a request to make of him?

78. One of David and Bathsheba's children would be listed in the genealogy of Jesus; another would be among the ancestors of Joseph, Jesus' earthly father. Look up the following verses and write down their names.

Matthew 1:6

Luke 3:31

Bathsheba

Short Essay Questions

 1. In ancient times, people often used their rooftops as part of their living area. We don't know if it was common for them to bathe there, but that's where Bathsheba was the night David first saw her. Once he determined who she was (and that she was married to one of his soldiers who was away at war), he sent messengers to bring her to his palace, where he committed adultery with her. Who put this temptation in front of David? Knowing this, list any actions that David and Bathsheba could have taken to prevent this sin. How can you resist when Satan tempts you to sin?

2. Re-read 2 Samuel 11:26, 12:10 and 12:15. What phrase is used to describe Bathsheba? Note that in verse 15, Bathsheba was married to David, and yet she is described the same way as in the other two verses. Now re-read 2 Samuel 12:24. By what name is she called in that verse? Finally, read Matthew 1:6 to see how she is referred to in Jesus' genealogy. What conclusion can you draw from these descriptions?

Bathsheba

3. On first reading of this story, it's hard to determine whether both David and Bathsheba were at fault for committing adultery, or whether only David was to blame. After all, the king could command someone to come to the castle, and they would have to obey. So Bathsheba may not have had a choice about coming to see David, or even about committing adultery with him. We don't know what was going on in her heart, but God knew. Now, re-read 2 Samuel 12:1-14, noting to whom God sent Nathan with this message, then keep score of how many times David is accused of sin, and how many times Bathsheba is accused of sin. Also, who was the "lamb" in Nathan's story? Does this affect your opinion of Bathsheba's behavior? Why or why not?

4. God convicted David of his sin, and David owned up to it (David's admission and repentance are detailed in his own words in Psalm 51). But that was not the end of the incident; God punished David, and as a result Bathsheba also suffered. Can you think of a time when you sinned and your punishment affected not just you, but others too? How did you feel?

5. Note how King Solomon, king of all Israel, reacts to the arrival of his mother in 1 Kings 2:19-20. As powerful as he was, he still treated his mother like royalty. List ten ways you can show love and respect to your mother.

Bathsheba

Discussion Starters for Mothers and Daughters

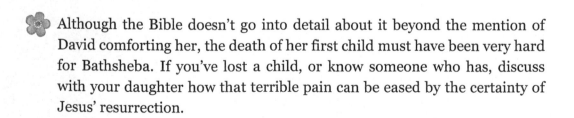

By the time David was old, Bathsheba was just one of his many wives, and held no special place of honor with him. Yet she was willing to go to him and remind him of his promise to make their son Solomon the next king. She went to the defense of her grown son, and the result was that he received his crown. Think of a time when you've come to the defense of one of your children and tell your daughter about it. Will there ever come a time when you won't want to defend your child? Explain to your daughter how that desire to protect a child is present from the moment you find out you're expecting.

Although the Bible doesn't go into detail about it beyond the mention of David comforting her, the death of her first child must have been very hard for Bathsheba. If you've lost a child, or know someone who has, discuss with your daughter how that terrible pain can be eased by the certainty of Jesus' resurrection.

Despite the sinful beginning of David and Bathsheba's relationship, God allowed two of their sons to be listed in the New Testament among Jesus' ancestors. As a mother, you know that God has a plan for each of your children's lives. Talk with your daughter about the things mothers must do to raise children who are open to being used by God now and in the future. Remind her that such things will be her responsibility if she has children.

 Two decisions (Bathsheba's decision to take a bath and David's decision to go for a late-night walk) resulted in changing Bathsheba from the wife of a soldier to the wife of one king and (eventually) the mother of another. She could never have dreamed that thousands of years later, people would know her name and her story....and it all began with those two decisions. Discuss with your daughter how even the most trivial decisions can sometimes have consequences that reach farther than we could ever imagine. Where can we go for guidance when we make decisions?

Notes:

Bathsheba

The Shunammite Woman

2 Kings 4 and 8
Time Period: 850-800 BC

Elisha was the successor to the prophet Elijah. A witness to Elijah being taken up to heaven, Elisha was given a double portion of Elijah's spirit and was able to perform miracles. In the beginning of 2 Kings, Elisha used his God-given power to heal the water at Jericho, bring water to the Desert of Edom, and provide a widow with a very productive jar of oil. In 2 Kings 4, he used power from God to help a Shunammite woman.

 Read 2 Kings 4:8-17, then answer the following questions:

1. To what town did Elisha go?

2. Elisha met a woman there; how is she described?

3. What did she offer him?

4. What became Elisha's habit after that?

5. What did she tell her husband about Elisha?

6. What did she decide to do for Elisha?

7. How did Elisha react to this?

8. Who summoned the Shunammite woman to see Elisha?

9. What did Elisha ask the woman?

10. Did she come up with something he could do for her?

11. What did Gehazi suggest?

The Shunammite Woman

12. What did Elisha predict would happen to her?

13. How did the Shunammite woman react to this prediction?

14. Was Elisha's prediction accurate?

Read 2 Kings 4:18-25

15. What did the child tell his father when he went out into the field to see him?

16. How did his father react?

17. What happened to the boy?

18. How did his mother react?

19. What did the woman ask her husband to do?

20. Did she tell her husband why she wanted to see Elisha?

21. What did she tell her husband before she left?

22. Did she take her time going to find Elisha?

23. Did she find Elisha?

❀——— **Read 2 Kings 4:26-37**

24. How did Elisha react when he saw the Shunammite woman coming towards him?

25. What questions did Elisha have?

26. What did the Shunammite woman do once she reached Elisha?

27. How did Gehazi respond?

28. What did Elisha then tell Gehazi?

29. What did the Shunammite woman finally say to Elisha?

30. Elisha reacted immediately to the woman's comments; what did he do?

31. Did the Shunammite woman want Elisha to go back with her?

The Shunammite Woman

32. Did he go back?

33. When Gehazi put Elisha's staff on the boy's face, how did the boy react?

34. What three things did Elisha do when he reached his room?

35. After he walked back and forth in the house, what did Elisha do?

36. How did the boy react?

37. After that, what did Elisha tell Gehazi to do?

38. How did the Shunammite woman react to what she saw?

Read 2 Kings 8:1-6

39. What had Elisha told the Shunammite woman to do?

40. What was his reason for telling her that?

41. Did she do what Elisha told her to do?

42. Where did the Shunammite woman and her family go?

43. How long did they live there?

44. Where did they go after that?

45. Whom did the Shunammite woman visit when they arrived?

46. Why did she visit him?

47. What was he doing when she got there?

48. What question had he asked just before the Shunammite woman arrived?

49. What story was the servant telling when the Shunammite woman got there?

50. How did the servant introduce the Shunammite woman?

51. What did the king say to the Shunammite woman?

The Shunammite Woman

52. How did she respond?

53. What did the king do for the Shunammite woman?

Short Essay Questions

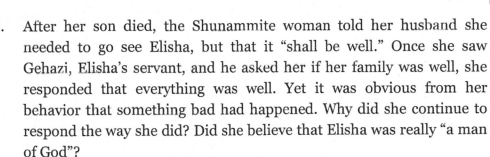

1. After her son died, the Shunammite woman told her husband she needed to go see Elisha, but that it "shall be well." Once she saw Gehazi, Elisha's servant, and he asked her if her family was well, she responded that everything was well. Yet it was obvious from her behavior that something bad had happened. Why did she continue to respond the way she did? Did she believe that Elisha was really "a man of God"?

The Shunammite Woman

2. The story of Elisha and the Shunammite woman shares many
    similarities with the story of Elisha's predecessor, Elijah, and the
    widow from Zarephath (1 Kings 17:7-24). Read that story, then list
    below the similarities between it and the Shunammite woman's
    experience.

3. In 2 Kings 8, Elisha told the Shunammite woman that she and her family should leave their country because a famine was coming, one that would last for seven years. She followed his direction; why do you think she did so?

4. The Shunammite woman arrived to see the king just as Gehazi was telling him the story of how Elisha had restored her son's life. Some people would say that this was a coincidence. In your opinion, *was* it a coincidence? Why or why not? Is there such a thing as coincidence?

The Shunammite Woman

Discussion Starters for Mothers and Daughters

When Elisha told the Shunammite woman that she would soon have a son, her response was not one of joy; instead, she told him not to mislead her, or to get her hopes up. This indicates that she had probably been disappointed before. Perhaps she had not been able to get pregnant, or she had suffered a miscarriage or stillbirth. Describe for your daughter a time when you had very high hopes for something that didn't happen the way you'd hoped. How did you deal with your disappointment? How do we know that God knows our disappointments? What does it mean when He doesn't let us have something we want very badly?

The Shunammite woman didn't have to tell Elijah that her son had died; he saw by her reaction that something terrible had happened. How can we be sensitive to the needs of others? How can we react properly to someone who is in emotional pain or even devastation? Look up and read the following Bible verses together: Job 16:5, Matthew 5:4, Luke 10:27, John 11:33-35 and 13:34. How can these verses help you know what to do?

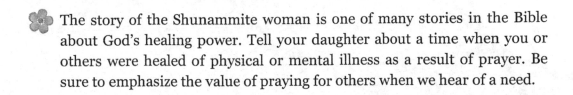

The story of the Shunammite woman is one of many stories in the Bible about God's healing power. Tell your daughter about a time when you or others were healed of physical or mental illness as a result of prayer. Be sure to emphasize the value of praying for others when we hear of a need.

The Shunammite woman and her family had to leave their home for seven years because of an impending famine. But when they returned, God gave them back not only the home and land they had lost, but also the income their land had generated in their absence; in other words, He gave back even more than the Shunammite woman had asked for. Tell your daughter about a time when God gave you back even more than you hoped for, whether after financial difficulties or simply in answer to prayer.

Notes:

The Shunammite Woman

Jezebel

1 and 2 Kings
Time Period: 874-841 BC

The story of Jezebel takes place during the same time period in which the Shunammite woman and her family lived. In fact, you'll find that a central character from the Shunammite woman's life also played a role in Jezebel's life.

Read 1 Kings 16:29-31, then answer the following questions:

1.   Who became king of Israel?

2.   How long would he reign over Israel?

3. How does verse 30 describe his behavior as king?

4. Verse 31 equates his sinfulness (and lack of concern about it) with something else he did; what was it?

Read 1 Kings 18:1-4

5. What did God tell his prophet Elijah to do?

6. Did Elijah obey God?

7. Was there a famine in Samaria (the place where Ahab lived while he ruled over Israel)?

8. Whom did Ahab summon for help in dealing with the famine?

9. What was Obadiah's regular job?

10. What else does the story mention about Obadiah besides his occupation?

11. What had Jezebel been doing?

Jezebel

12. How had Obadiah reacted to Jezebel's actions?

Obadiah helped King Ahab by going out in the countryside to find grass to feed the king's horses and mules (the drought made it hard for them to find green grass to eat). While out walking, he met up with the prophet Elijah, someone Ahab had been hunting for because Elijah had bluntly pointed out to Ahab his sins against God. Elijah challenged Ahab and his false prophets to a contest between Baal and the true and only God, which Baal naturally lost. Elijah then slaughtered all the false prophets, after which God sent rain on the land. Meanwhile, Ahab ran home to his wife Jezebel.

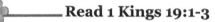

Read 1 Kings 19:1-3

13. What did Ahab do when he arrived home?

14. How did Jezebel react to Ahab's news?

15. What was Elijah's reaction to the message he received?

Elijah ran to the desert, where he asked God to take his life, saying he'd had enough. But God instead sent an angel to care for him, then had a conversation with Elijah during which he instructed him to find and anoint Elisha, who would become his assistant and eventually succeed him as prophet.

Read 1 Kings 21:1-16

16. What did Ahab ask of Naboth, the vineyard owner?

17. How did Naboth respond to Ahab's request?

18. What did Ahab do when he got home?

19. When Ahab told Jezebel what had happened, what was her response?

20. What did Jezebel do then?

21. Who helped Jezebel with her plan?

22. Who sent word to Jezebel that Naboth had been killed?

23. What did Jezebel do once she got the news of Naboth's death?

24. Did Ahab obey Jezebel?

Read 1 Kings 21:17-29

25. What did God tell Elijah to do?

26. Where did God say Elijah would find Ahab?

Jezebel

27. What two things did God tell Elijah to say to Ahab?

28. How did Ahab greet Elijah?

29. List the things Elijah told Ahab he would do to him.

30. Why did Elijah say he would do these things?

31. What did Elijah predict about Ahab's wife Jezebel?

32. Verses 25-26 give the reasons why Ahab would be punished by God through Elijah. What were the reasons, and who else was implicated in these sins?

33. How did Ahab react to Elijah's words?

34. What did God say to Elijah regarding Ahab's reaction?

King Ahab eventually died in battle, making Jezebel a widow. Meanwhile, God took Elijah up to heaven in a whirlwind, leaving Elisha to take over as God's prophet to Israel. Elisha later assigned a young prophet to anoint Jehu as the new king of Israel, and told Jehu exactly what God wanted him to do.

Read 2 Kings 9:6-10

35. When the young prophet anointed Jehu, what was the first thing he told Jehu that God wanted him to do?

36. Why did God want Jehu to do those things?

37. Would God spare any of Ahab's house?

38. What did God say would happen to Jezebel?

 Read 2 Kings 9:30-37

39. What did Jezebel do when she heard Jehu had arrived in Jezreel?

40. How did she greet Jehu when he arrived?

41. What did Jehu then ask her servants?

42. What happened next?

43. What happened to Jezebel's body?

Jezebel

44. What did Jehu do then?

45. What did the servants find when they went to bury Jezebel?

46. When Jehu heard what the servants found, he referred to a prediction by Elijah; what was it?

Short Essay Questions

1. In 1 Kings 21:4, King Ahab reacted to Naboth's refusal to sell a vineyard to him by sulking and pouting on his bed and refusing to eat. We can laugh at this childish behavior coming from a king, of all people, but the reality is that many people sulk when things don't go their way. Look up the following verses and use them to answer this question: How should we react when we're denied something we want? See Matthew 6:8, Romans 8:28, James 3:14-16, and 4:1-3.

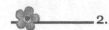

2. Jezebel was so eager to promote her false gods among the Israelites that she had God's prophets killed, although she did not commit the actual murders. Later, when she decided to get rid of Naboth so her husband could have his vineyard, she used her position to order people to frame Naboth so that he would be punished (put to death) for something he didn't do. In both cases, she didn't get her hands dirty by doing the actual killing. Was she guilty of murder? Why or why not?

3. Jezebel is the most evil woman in the Bible; she's an example of everything God does *not* want women to be. Her polar opposite is the woman described in Proverbs 31. Read Proverbs 31:10-31, then list her many attributes. (Note the irony in what verse 31 suggests should happen to her at the city gate as opposed to what happened to Jezebel at the city gate in 2 Kings 9:31-37).

Jezebel

Discussion Starters for Mothers and Daughters

In 1 Kings 21:25, we read that Ahab was encouraged to do evil by his wife Jezebel. We know that encouraging evil is a sin; Jezebel was an "encouragement" to her husband, but the wrong kind. How should a godly wife encourage her husband? What types of encouragement is he likely to need?

When Jezebel heard that Jehu was coming to town, she put on makeup and fixed her hair. Explain to your daughter how some women use their looks in an effort to manipulate men, and why our daughters must be careful (with their appearance and behavior) so that young men don't misinterpret their appearance.

Notes:

Esther

Esther 1 to 10
Time Period: 483-473 BC

The book of Esther tells the story of a brave young Jewish woman living in Persia (present day Iran) who risks her life to save her people. This book is one of only two in the Bible named after women; the other is Ruth.

 Read Esther 1:1-9, then answer the following questions:

1. What was the name of the king?

2. How large was his kingdom, and how far did it extend?

3. Where did this king live?

4. What did he do during his third year as king?

5. What did he display during this time?

6. For how long did he do this?

7. How long was the banquet?

8. Describe the decorations for the banquet.

9. How was the wine served at the banquet?

10. Who was the king's wife, and what did she do during the banquet?

Read Esther 1:10-22

11. What kind of mood was the king in by the seventh day of the banquet?

12. Who was commanded to do something by the king? What was the command?

Esther

13. Why did the king make this command?

14. Was his command obeyed?

15. Did that bother the king?

16. What did the king do about this?

17. What was he told?

18. What was expected to be the effect of the queen's behavior?

19. What action did the experts recommend?

20. What did the experts expect would be the result of this?

21. How did the king and his nobles feel about the experts' advice?

Read Esther 2:1-4

22. When did the king remember the queen's behavior and his subsequent decree?

23. What did his attendants suggest to him?

24. What would be done with those they found?

25. What would be the purpose of this?

26. What was the king's reaction to this suggestion?

Read Esther 2:5-11

27. How did Mordecai end up in Susa?

28. What was his cousin's name, and how did he happen to be living with her?

29. How is she described in verse 7?

30. Where was she taken?

31. What was Hegai's opinion of her?

32. What did Hegai do for her?

Esther

33. Did anyone in the palace or harem know of her background? Why or why not?

34. What was Mordecai doing during this time?

Read Esther 2:12-18

35. What kind of preparation was required before each girl was ready to be sent to the king?

36. What was each girl allowed to take with her when she went to the king's palace?

37. When would each girl go to see the king?

38. How would a girl know she had pleased the king?

39. What did Esther ask to bring with her when it was her turn to visit the king?

40. How did everyone feel about Esther?

41. When did Esther finally visit the king?

42. What did the king think about Esther?

43. What did the king do for Esther?

44. Name three ways the king celebrated this event.

Read Esther 2:19-23

45. Who was sitting at the king's gate?

46. Did anyone at the palace know that Esther was Jewish?

47. How had Esther obeyed Mordecai in this situation?

48. What important information did Mordecai overhear?

49. How did Mordecai react to this news?

50. What was the result of Mordecai's action?

51. Was Mordecai rewarded for this?

Esther

52. Where was this incident recorded?

Read Esther 3:1-15

53. Who was honored by the king?

54. Why was he honored?

55. How did King Xerxes honor him?

56. What did the officials at the king's gate do?

57. Why did they do this?

58. Who refused to do this?

59. Why did he refuse to do this?

60. What did the royal officials do about his refusal?

61. Why did they do this?

62. What was Haman's reaction?

63. Whom did Haman want to punish?

64. What was the *pur*?

65. What did Haman do once the *pur* was cast?

66. How did Haman suggest those who fulfilled the king's decree be rewarded?

67. How did the king react to Haman's plan?

68. Describe the decree Haman suggested to the King.

69. Who received written notice of this decree?

70. Re-read Esther 1:1; how many provinces did Xerxes rule?

71. How were the written notices of the decree sealed?

Esther

72. Why were the written notices sent out?

73. How did the citizens of Susa feel about the decree?

Read Esther 4:1-11

74. How did Mordecai react to the decree?

75. How far did he go into the city?

76. How did the Jews in all the provinces react?

77. Who told Esther about Mordecai?

78. What did Esther do once she found out?

79. Did Mordecai do as Esther wished?

80. Did Esther know why Mordecai was acting the way he was?

81. What did Esther do next?

82. What occurred when the eunuch met with Mordecai?

83. Where did the eunuch go after meeting with Mordecai?

84. What message did Esther send to Mordecai?

Read Esther 4:12-17

85. How did Mordecai respond to Esther?

86. What did he suggest would happen if she remained silent?

87. What important idea did his message suggest?

88. What was Esther's reply to Mordecai?

89. What would she be doing during that time?

90. What did Esther say she would do at the end of three days?

91. Did Esther understand the risk she was taking? Explain.

Esther

92. Did Mordecai do as Esther asked?

Read Esther 5:1-8

93. How did Esther prepare herself before approaching the king?

94. What did the king do when he saw Esther in the inner court?

95. How did Esther react?

96. What did the king tell her she could have?

97. How did Esther respond?

98. What was the king's response to Esther's request?

99. Did he do what he said he would do?

100. What did the king say to Esther while they were drinking wine?

101. What was Esther's response to the king?

Read Esther 5:9-14

102. What kind of mood was Haman in when he left the banquet?

103. What soon changed Haman's mood?

104. Did Haman do anything about his observation?

105. What did Haman do when he got home?

106. What special honors did he announce to his audience?

107. What did he say took away his satisfaction regarding these honors?

108. What suggestion did his wife and friends make regarding how he should deal with Mordecai?

109. Did Haman follow their suggestion?

Read Esther 6:1-10

110. In the first verse, what problem did King Xerxes have?

Esther

111. How did he try to solve his problem?

112. What did he learn?

113. What did he ask his attendants after learning this?

114. What was the response of the attendants?

115. What was the king's next question?

116. Who was in the court, and for what reason?

117. What was the attendants' answer to the king's question?

118. What did the king then command?

119. With what question did the king greet Haman?

120. What did Haman think about the king's question?

121. How did Haman answer the king?

122. Did the king like Haman's idea?

123. What did the king order Haman to do?

124. Did he want Haman to leave anything out of his suggested method?

Read Esther 6:11-14

125. Did Haman obey the king?

126. What exactly did Haman have to do?

127. How did Haman react after he was finished?

128. What advice did his wife and friends give him?

129. How was their conversation with Haman interrupted?

Esther

Read Esther 7:1-10

130. Who attended Esther's banquet?

131. What did the king ask Esther while they were drinking wine?

132. What two important things did he tell her?

133. What was Esther's answer to the king's question?

134. How did Esther elaborate on her request?

135. What did she say would *not* have warranted her bothering the king?

136. How did the king react to Esther's news?

137. Whom did Esther say was responsible for the danger she was in, and how did she describe this person?

138. How did Haman react to the king and queen's discussion?

139. Where did the king go, and why?

140. What did Haman decide to do?

141. What was going on between Esther and Haman when the king came back?

142. How did the king respond to this sight?

143. What was then done to Haman?

144. What helpful information did the eunuch Harbona offer?

145. What happened to Haman?

146. What was the king's reaction to Haman's fate?

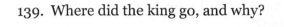 **Read Esther 8:1-8**

147. What did the king give Esther on the day that Haman died?

Esther

148. What did the king do for Mordecai once he found out that Mordecai was Esther's cousin and guardian?

149. What did Esther then do for Mordecai?

150. Describe Esther's next request of the king.

151. Was the king willing to hear Esther's request this time?

152. What did Esther specifically ask the king to do?

153. How did the king answer Esther?

In Esther 8:9-9:10, we learn that Mordecai wrote a new decree granting all Jews in the king's 127 provinces the right to defend themselves, including the right to kill anyone who might attack them. That would also give them the right to keep the property of their attackers. They were given a certain day to do this. The decree was sent immediately to every province (on fast horses belonging to the king). Jews throughout the kingdom celebrated this decree, and many non-Jews became Jews because they didn't want the Jews to counter-attack them as they were now allowed to do.

On the prescribed day, the Jews attacked and killed those who had tried to destroy them, including Haman's ten sons. But they didn't take the possessions of those they killed, even though that was traditionally the right of conquerors. Mordecai told the Jews they should celebrate their victory over their enemies every year, so that it wouldn't be forgotten by their descendants. Even today, Jews celebrate this event, which is called Purim because of the lot, or *pur*, that had been cast against them by Haman. Mordecai was made second in command after King Xerxes, but it was Queen Esther who officially authorized Purim. She's remembered to this day as the woman who risked her life for her people.

Esther

Short Essay Questions

1. PART A: Esther spent a year being prepared to become a wife fit for a king. For what are you being prepared? Look up the following verses for some clues:

   Psalm 138:8

   Mark 13:10

   Mark 16:15

   John 6:27-29

John 14:2

1 Timothy 2:9-15

1 Timothy 3:11

1 Timothy 4:7-8

Titus 2:4-5

Revelation 21:1-4

Esther

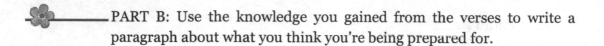

PART B: Use the knowledge you gained from the verses to write a paragraph about what you think you're being prepared for.

2. Haman thought he had the perfect plan for getting rid of not only Mordecai, but *all* the Jews. Yet God used the gallows that Haman intended for Mordecai to do away with Haman himself. Proverbs 19:21 states, "There are many devices in a man's heart; nevertheless the counsel of the Lord, that shall stand." What can we learn from this?

Esther

3. Haman was full of pride, so much so that when Mordecai did not bow down to him after the king honored him, Haman actually became enraged, and came up with his evil plan. The book of Proverbs gives us some insight regarding pride. Look up the following verses and explain how God feels about pride; note also what attitude God prefers us to have instead of pride.

Proverbs 8:13

Proverbs 11:2

Proverbs 13:10

Proverbs 14:3

Proverbs 16:18

Proverbs 29:23

What attitude does God prefer, as mentioned in some of those verses?

4. The book of Esther is unusual in that God is never mentioned in it, yet it's clear that He acted in Esther's life, and that He used her and others in her sphere to protect His people. Look up the following verses and list how God was involved in each:

Esther 1:12

Esther 1:19

Esther 2:5-6

Esther 2:8-9

Esther 2:16-17

Esther

Esther 2:21-22

Esther 5:2

Esther 6:1-2

Esther 7:7-8

Esther 8:2

_____ 5. If Esther had chosen not to bother the king with her concerns, would all of the Jews have been murdered due to Haman's decree? See Esther 4:14.

Esther

Discussion Starters for Mothers and Daughters

Esther did not demand that the king save her people; she humbly and patiently put a plan into effect to ask him. Share with your daughter how you've used this method in your life, and how she can use it when she has a need or want.

Once Esther was living in the king's palace, both in the harem and later as his wife and queen, she didn't have to answer to her guardian Mordecai anymore. Yet she obeyed his commands to keep her Jewish heritage a secret, and to act before Haman could kill all of the Jews; her obedience saved her life as well as the lives of many others. Can you think of a time when you heeded the advice of a parent or other elder after you became an adult, and how it benefited you? Share any such stories with your daughter.

Review Short Essay Question #4, noting all the ways that God's hand worked in Esther's life, even though the book never specifically mentions Him doing so. Looking back over your own life so far, can you see God's hand in different events, even though you might not have realized it until afterwards? Share these stories with your daughter, and use them to encourage her that He's working in her life too, even if she doesn't see Him doing so.

Esther

Answer Key

Eve

Genesis 1:26-31

1. Jesus and the Holy Spirit were there at the beginning. (verse 26)
2. God (verse 27)
3. He blessed them. (verse 28)
4. He told them to 1) be fruitful and increase in number, 2) fill the earth and subdue it, and 3) rule over fish, birds and every living creature. (verse 28)
5. Both of them (verse 28)
6. To have children (verse 28)
7. Every seed-bearing plant and every tree that has fruit with seed in it (verse 29)

Genesis 2:1-25

8. From the dust of the ground (verse 7)
9. God breathed into his nostrils. (verse 7)
10. A garden (verse 8)
11. In Eden (verse 8)
12. Trees that were nice to look at and good to eat from (verse 9)
13. The tree of life and the tree of the knowledge of good and evil (verse 9)
14. To work the garden and take care of it (verse 15)
15. To eat from any tree except from the tree of the knowledge of good and evil (verses 16-17)
16. He would die. (verse 17)
17. A helper suitable for him (verse 18)
18. God brought beasts and birds to Adam and he named them. (verse 19)
19. No (verse 20)
20. God put Adam in a deep sleep, took one of his ribs and used it to make a woman, then brought her to Adam. (verses 21-22)

21. Woman (verse 23)
22. Adam (verse 23)
23. She is part of him, or one with him; the two of them are as one person. (verse 23)
24. Marriage
25. In marriage, God joins a man and a woman and they become one. God created marriage when He created Eve and declared that she and Adam were one.
26. They had nothing to hide or be ashamed of. (verse 25)

Genesis 3: 1-7
27. The serpent (verse 1)
28. "Did God really say, 'You must not eat from any tree in the garden'?" (verse 1)
29. She told the serpent that God said not to eat from or touch the tree in the middle of the garden, or they would die. (verse 3)
30. It told her that she wouldn't die, and that God knew that if she and Adam ate the fruit of that tree, they would be like Him. (verses 4-5)
31. She took some of the forbidden fruit and ate it, and gave some to Adam, who also ate it. (verse 6)
32. No
33. Their eyes were opened (they became aware of their sin) and they realized they were naked, so they sewed fig leaves together to cover themselves. (verse 7)
34. Adam (Gen. 2:15-17)
35. Adam, because God had told him directly not to eat from that tree, but he didn't stop the woman from eating the fruit, and even accepted some from her and ate it. (verse 6)
36. No

Genesis 3:8-24
37. They heard God walking. (verse 8)
38. They hid in the trees. (verse 8)

Eve

39. They were afraid because they had disobeyed God. (verse 8)

40. No

41. Adam (verse 10)

42. Adam said, "I heard you in the garden, and I was afraid because I was naked; so I hid." (verse 10)

43. God wanted to see if Adam would be honest with him. (verse 11)

44. He blamed Eve, and also God ("...the woman *you* put here with me...".) (verse 12)

45. She blamed the serpent. (verse 13)

46. All three of them: Adam, the woman, and the serpent (verses 14 through 19)

47. God cursed the serpent, forcing it to crawl on its belly and eat dust all the days of its life. (verse 14)

48. Definition of enmity: deep hatred, as between enemies
    1. Jesus is the woman's offspring/seed.
    2. The serpent's (or Satan's) offspring/seed are his agents whose purpose is to turn people away from God.

49. He is saying that Jesus will overcome death and Satan.

50. God told the woman she would have increased pain in childbirth, and that she would look to her husband, who would rule over her. (verse 16)

51. God told Adam that because he listened to his wife and therefore disobeyed God's command to him, the ground would be cursed and hard to work, but Adam would have to work it anyway to grow food (no more free and plentiful food as there was in the Garden) until the day he died. (verse 17-19)

52. Adam would eventually die, be buried, and decompose back into the earth from which God originally formed him.

53. Adam named the woman Eve. (verse 20)

54. He named her Eve because it means "living," and Eve would become the mother of all the living; she is everyone's original female ancestor.

55. Jesus

56. He made clothes for them, so they would be protected out in the world. (verse 21)

57. He says that Adam must not be allowed to eat from the tree, and live forever. (verse 22)

58. He banished Adam and Eve from the Garden of Eden. They would have to work hard to grow their own food and provide their own shelter. (verse 23)

59. God put cherubim (angels) and a flaming sword that flashed back and forth at the front of the Garden of Eden to guard the way to the tree of life. (verse 24)

Genesis 4:1-16

60. Eve said her son came "from the LORD." (verse 1)

61. Abel (verse 2)

62. Cain became jealous of Abel because God looked more favorably on Abel's offering. Cain murdered Abel, and then lied about it to God. Cain was then banished to live out of God's presence. (verses 3-16)

63. God said if anyone ever killed Cain they would "suffer vengeance seven times over." He then put a mark on Cain so that no one would kill him. (verse 15)

64. Seth (verse 25)

Short Essay Questions

1. Answers may vary.
2. Answers may vary.
3. Both working on and caring for the earth should be mentioned.
4. Diagram should look similar to this:

God

⇧

Christ

⇧

Man

⇧

Woman

Eve

Essay should include some mention of divorce being against God's wishes, and of how God wants husbands and wives to treat each other.

5. Satan didn't direct Eve to eat the fruit; he lured her into doing it. Make sure the answer includes mention of resisting Satan as well as asking God through prayer for help in resisting temptation.

6. Answers may vary.

7. Answers may vary.

8. Answers may vary, but should include a reference to the fact that we are no better than Adam and Eve.

9. Remorse should be a main element of the answer.

Sarah

Genesis 11:27-32

1. Sarai (verse 29)
2. That she was barren; she had no children. (verse 30)
3. He intended to take them to Canaan, but they settled in Haran. (verse 31)

Genesis 12:1-9

4. He told Abram to leave Haran to go to the land He would show him. (verse 1)
5. God promised to make Abram into a great nation, to bless him and make his name great, to make him be a blessing, to bless those who blessed Abram, to curse whoever cursed Abram, and to bless all people on earth through him. (verses 2-3)
6. Yes (verse 4)
7. 75 years old (verse 4)
8. The Bible doesn't tell how old Sarai was at that time.
9. Canaan (verse 5)
10. God promised to give the land to Abram's offspring. (verse 7)
11. No (verse 5, also Genesis 11:30)
12. It implied that Abram would eventually become a father.

Genesis 12:10 to 13:2

13. There was a famine in Canaan. (verse 10)
14. He warned her that because of her beauty, the Egyptians might kill him in order to have her. He told her to tell the Egyptians she was his sister. (verses 11-13)
15. He was asking her to lie.
16. They saw that she was a very beautiful woman. (verse 14)

17. She was taken to the Pharaoh's palace. (verse 15)
18. He gave Abram sheep and cattle, donkeys, servants and camels. (verse 16)
19. He planned to take Abram's "sister" to be one of his wives. (verse 19)
20. God inflicted serious diseases on Pharaoh and his household. (verse 17)
21. God wanted Pharaoh to send Sarai back to Abram.
22. Sarai could not become Pharaoh's wife because she was already married to Abram. (Also, God planned to send Abram offspring through Sarah.)
23. He summoned Abram and asked him why he said Sarai was his sister instead of his wife. Then he told Abram to take Sarai and go. (verse 19)
24. They went to the south (Negeb). (verse 1)
25. He had become very wealthy. (verse 2)
26. His wealth had come at least partly from Pharaoh—re-read Genesis 12:16.

Genesis 15:1-6
27. The Lord (verse 1)
28. He said he was childless and had no heir, and that a servant would get everything. (verse 2-3)
29. God promised Abram he would have a son of his own. (verse 4)
30. God promised Abram he would have as many descendants as there are stars. (verse 5)
31. Yes (verse 6)
32. She would have a child.

Genesis 16:1-15
33. Hagar (verse 1)
34. She asked him to sleep with Hagar so Sarai could build a family through her. (verse 2)
35. She knew God had promised Abram children from his body. Since she couldn't have children, she thought this would make God's promise of descendants come true. (verse 2, and also Gen. 15:4-5)
36. Yes (verses 2-4)
37. She became pregnant with Abram's child. (verse 4)
38. She despised Sarai. (verse 4)
39. Hagar felt superior to Sarai because she could have Abram's child and Sarai could not.

40. She blamed Abram. (verses 5-6)
41. He gave her permission to do what she thought best. (verse 6)
42. She mistreated her. (verse 6)
43. She ran away. (verse 6)
44. The angel of the Lord (verse 7)
45. He told Hagar to go back to Sarai and submit to her. (verse 9)
46. He promised her that she would have too many descendants to count. (verse 10)
47. He said she would soon have a son whom she should name Ishmael, that the Lord was giving him to her because He heard of her misery, and that Ishmael would be a "wild donkey of a man" who would have a hard time getting along with people. (verses 11-12)
48. "The God who sees me" (verse 13)
49. She bore Abram's son Ishmael.
50. Abram was 86. (verse 16)

Genesis 17:15-22
51. Sarah (verse 15)
52. God said he would give her a son, and that she would become the mother of nations. (verse 16)
53. He fell facedown and laughed. (verse 17)
54. He laughed at the idea of him being 100 and Sarah being 90 and the two of them finally having a son. (verse 17)
55. He said that Sarah would have a son that they should name Isaac (verse 19)
56. It would happen by the same time the following year.

Genesis 18:1-15
57. Three men (verse 2)
58. He told her to bake bread (verse 6)
59. They asked, "Where is your wife?" (verse 9)
60. The Lord spoke. The men were messengers from God.
61. The message was that the Lord would come back in about a year and Sarah would have a son.

Sarah

62. She laughed to herself at the thought that she could have a child in her old age. (verse 12)
63. The Lord (verse 13)
64. He asked if anything was too hard for the Lord, and then repeated that He would be back at the appointed time the next year, and that Sarah would have a son. (verse 14)
65. Afraid (verse 15)
66. She lied and said she did not laugh. (verse 15)
67. He said "Yes, you did laugh." (verse 15)

Genesis 20:1-18

68. Just as he did in Egypt, he told people Sarah was his sister. (verses 1-2)
69. To take Sarah for his wife (verse 2)
70. God came to Abimelech in a dream and told him he was as good as dead because he had just taken Sarah, a married woman. (verse 3))
71. He told God he had not gone near Sarah, and that he had a clear conscience. (verses 4-5)
72. God said He knew Abimelech had a clear conscience, so He kept him from sinning against Him. (verse 6)
73. He told him to return Sarah to Abraham or he and his household would die. (verse 7)
74. In a dream God gave to Abimelech (verses 3-7)
75. He told his officials what had happened, and they got scared. Then he asked Abraham why he had lied to him. (verses 8-9)
76. The same way he did in Egypt; he said he was afraid so he told Sarah to lie and say Abraham was her brother (verses 11-13)
77. He gave Abraham livestock and slaves, returned Sarah to him, let him live where he wanted, and gave him shekels (money). (verses 14-16)
78. He prayed to God, who then healed Abimelech and his household, who couldn't have children because God sealed up all their wombs once Abimelech took Sarah. (verses 17-18)

Genesis 21: 1-7

79. She became pregnant and had a son. (verses 1-2)
80. "...at the set time of which God had spoken to him"

81. He named the baby Isaac.
82. He circumcised Isaac when he was eight days old.
83. 100 years old (verse 5)
84. She laughed again, but this time with joy. (verse 6-7)

Genesis 21:8-12

85. Wean: to train a child to stop nursing and take other food. Once Isaac was weaned, Abraham held a great feast. (verse 8)
86. Ishmael, who was mocking them (verse 9)
87. She told Abraham to get rid of Hagar and Ishmael because Ishmael would never share Isaac's inheritance. (verse 10)
88. It distressed Abraham because it concerned his other son, Ishmael. (verse 11)
89. God told Abraham not to be so upset, and to listen to Sarah because it was through Isaac that his offspring would be reckoned. (verse 12)
90. God said Ishmael would also be made into a nation because of being Abraham's seed. (verse 13)

Genesis 23:1-2

91. 127 years old (verse 1)
92. He mourned and wept. (verse 2)
93. About 36 years

Short Essay Questions

1. God might not give a woman a child because He has other plans for her life, or because her gifts do not include the gift of mothering.
2. Answers should include a reference to God being more concerned about our hearts than an earthly standard of beauty.
3. Sarah would not have been taken by the Pharaoh, and he and his household would not have been stricken with plagues. The idea here is not to imply that being beautiful is bad, but that being beautiful is not always easy and can actually make life difficult at times.
4. Abram should have trusted God to protect him and Sarai, and could have also prayed to God to take away the spirit of fear, if necessary. Answer should include a personal interpretation of this.

Sarah

5. God does not need our help to fulfill His promises. Biblical examples of this are numerous; students might cite the primary example of God sending the Savior, but others could include God's protection of Isaac even after telling Abraham to sacrifice him, His protection of Joseph as he became a great leader, His promise to Noah (rainbow) that He would never again send floods over the entire earth, etc.

6. Answers will vary. The verse reminds us that we have many plans, but God's plans will prevail.

7. Sarai mistreated Hagar because she had become insolent; Sarai was probably also jealous of Hagar for being able to have a child. The rest of the answer will vary.

8. God always knows our thoughts; He made us. He was reminding them that He can do anything.

9. Answers will vary.

10. The other woman mentioned by name in the "Faith Hall of Fame" was Rahab; Jesus is a direct descendant of both women.

11. Answers will vary.

Rebekah

Genesis 24:1-14

1. The Canaanites (verse 3)
2. Abraham's relatives in his homeland (verse 4)
3. The servant wanted to know what he should do if the woman was unwilling to come back to Canaan with him, and whether he should then take Isaac back to Abraham's native country. (verse 5)
4. He did not want Isaac to go there. He wanted him to stay in the land God had promised to Abraham's offspring. (verse 7)
5. An angel (verse 7)
6. The servant would be released from his promise to Abraham to find a wife for Isaac from among Abraham's relatives. (verse 8)
7. He took ten of his master's camels, plus "goods of his master" which are not specified. (verse 10)
8. Nahor (verse 10)
9. He made the camels kneel down by a well of water. (verse 11)
10. He prayed to God for success in finding a wife for Isaac, and asked that he be shown the right young woman. He prayed that when he asked for a drink of water, the right girl would not only agree to do so, but would offer water for his camels, too. (verse 14)

Genesis 24:15-27

11. Rebekah came out to the spring with her jar on her shoulder. (verse 15)
12. Rebekah's grandfather Nahor and Isaac's father Abraham were brothers. (verse 15)

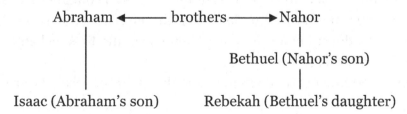

13. Very beautiful, a virgin, no man had ever lain with her. (verse 16)

14. He asked for a drink of water from her jar. (verse 17)

15. She gave him a drink, and then she offered to draw water for the camels, too, and did so. (verse 19-20)

16. He took out a gold ring and two gold bracelets. Note: these were to be given to and worn by the girl who would become Isaac's wife. (verse 22)

17. He asked her whose daughter she was and if there would be room in her father's house to spend the night. (Note: in those times, it was common to allow travelers to stay in one's home, since there were few other places for them to stay inside for the night) (verse 23)

18. He wanted to make sure Rebekah was related to Abraham, as Abraham had requested. (verse 4)

19. He bowed down and worshiped the Lord, thanking Him for leading him to Abraham's relatives. (verse 26-27)

Genesis 24:28-49

20. She ran to tell her mother's household what had happened. (verse 28)

21. Rebekah's brother Laban (verse 29)

22. When he saw that his sister was wearing the ring and bracelets, and heard her tell what the servant had said to her, he knew she was being offered marriage. (verse 30)

23. He offered him lodging, and food for him and his camels (verses 31-32)

24. He didn't want to eat until he had told Rebekah's family why he was there, who had sent him, and how God led him to them. (verses 33-48)

Genesis 24:50-61

25. He asked them whether or not they would show "kindness and faithfulness" to his master; in other words, would they or would they not allow him to take Rebekah back to Canaan to marry Isaac. (verse 49)

26. Laban and Bethuel told the servant that Rebekah could become Isaac's wife because the entire situation was from the Lord. (verse 50-51)

27. He bowed down before the Lord, then gave gifts to Rebekah and her family. (verse 52-53)

28. They asked him to give them ten more days with Rebekah. (verse 55)

29. No; he asked them not to detain him because he needed to get back to his master. (verse 56)

30. She said she would go. (verse 58)

31. Rebekah and the servant were accompanied by her nurse, her maids and some of Abraham's men who had traveled with the servant. (verses 59,61)

32. They blessed her, asking that she be given offspring ("thousands upon thousands") who would overcome their enemies. (verse 60)

Genesis 24:62-67

33. He had just come from Beer Lahai Roi, where he had been living in the Negev (the desert). (verse 62)

34. He went out into the field to meditate. (verse 63)

35. Rebekah, Abraham's servant, and the others traveling with them (verse 64)

36. She covered herself with her veil. (verse 65)

37. He brought Rebekah into the tent that had been his mother's, and married her. (verse 67)

38. He loved her. (verse 67)

39. He was comforted after his mother's death. (verse 67)

Genesis 25:19-26

40. Isaac was 40 years old. (verse 20)

41. Rebekah was barren. (verse 21)

42. Rebekah became pregnant with twins. (verse 21)

43. The babies were jostling each other within her. (verse 22)

44. He told her there were two nations within her, and one would be stronger than the other, and the older would serve the younger. (verse 23)

45. Rebekah gave birth to twin boys. The first was red and hairy, and they named him Esau. The second came out with his hand grasping Esau's heel, and they named him Jacob.

46. He was sixty years old. (verse 26)

47. He waited twenty years. (verses 26, 20)

Rebekah

Genesis 25:27-34

48. Esau was a skillful hunter and loved the open country. Jacob was quiet and stayed by the tents.

49. Isaac loved Esau, and Rebekah loved Jacob. (verse 28)

50. Jacob responded, "First sell me your birthright." (verses 30-31)

51. Esau said, "What good is the birthright to me?" (verse 32)

52. Jacob made Esau swear an oath that he was selling the birthright. (verse 33)

53. Jacob gave Esau some bread and some lentil stew. (verse 34)

54. The Bible says Esau despised his birthright. (verse 34)

Genesis 26:1-11

55. There was a famine. (verse 1)

56. God told him not to go to Egypt for food, but to stay in his land for a while and God would bless him. (verse 3)

57. Yes, he stayed in Gerar. (verse 6)

58. He told them she was his sister. (verse 7)

59. He was concerned that if the men knew Rebekah was his wife, they'd kill him so they could marry her because she was beautiful. (verse 7)

60. It happened twice to Abraham and Sarah, Isaac's parents. (see Genesis 12 and Genesis 20)

61. No, the king still questioned Isaac and asked why he had misled them about Rebekah, and pointed out that they might have sinned by taking her (verse 10), just as Pharaoh and a previous Abimelech said to Abraham.

62. He caused Abimelech to order protection for Isaac and Rebekah. (verse 11)

Genesis 26:12-13

63. He blessed Isaac by causing his crops to produce a hundredfold. (verse 12)

64. Isaac became very wealthy. (verse 13)

Genesis 26:34-35

65. Esau was forty years old. (verse 34)

66. He married Judith daughter of Beeri the Hittite, and also Basemath daughter of Elon the Hittite. (verse 34)
67. The women were a source of grief for Isaac and Rebekah. (verse 35)

Genesis 27:1-13

68. Isaac was getting old, and wanted to give Esau his blessing before he died. (verses 2-4)
69. Isaac asked Esau to hunt some wild game and prepare it for him. (verse 3-4)
70. Rebekah was listening. (verse 5)
71. Rebekah told Jacob what had gone on between Isaac and Esau. She also told Jacob to bring two choice young goats for her to prepare, so Jacob could bring them to Isaac and get the blessing before Isaac died. (verses 6-10)
72. It would be quicker for Jacob to take goats from their flock than to go out and hunt wild game like Esau did. Also, Jacob was not a hunter, so it would be a lot easier on him to bring goats.
73. Jacob immediately understood, because his first comment was how he would make his smooth skin feel like Esau's hairy skin, so he knew Rebekah wanted him to deceive his father. (verse 11-12)
74. Jacob was afraid his father would know he was tricking him, and would bring a curse on him instead of a blessing. (verse 12)
75. She said the curse would fall on her. (verse 13)

Genesis 27:13-29

76. Jacob got the goats so his mother could prepare them. Rebekah prepared the goats just the way Isaac liked them, put Esau's clothes on Jacob, and covered Jacob's smooth hands and neck with the goatskins. (verses 14-17)
77. Jacob did. (verse 18)
78. Jacob told Isaac he was "Esau your firstborn." (verse 19)
79. He touched him. (verse 22)
80. He thought he could, but he wasn't sure because it was Jacob's voice. (verse 22)
81. Isaac asked Jacob if he really was Esau, and Jacob said he was. (verse 24)

Rebekah

82. He asked for the game to eat so he could give his son the blessing. (verse 25)

83. He gave him the blessing. (verses 27-29)

84. Isaac said God would give him rain (heaven's dew) and good land (earth's richness), plenty of grain and wine, many nations to serve him and people to bow down to him, make him lord over his brothers and they would bow down to him, and also that those who cursed him would be cursed and those who blessed him would be blessed. (verses 27-29)

Genesis 27:30-40

85. Esau (verses 30-31)

86. Esau told his father to sit up and eat some of the food, so he could give Esau his blessing. (verse 31)

87. Isaac asked, "Who are you?" (verse 32)

88. He trembled violently. (verse 33)

89. Isaac told Esau that he had already given the blessing to someone else, and that person would indeed be blessed. (verse 33)

90. He burst out with a loud and bitter cry and asked to be blessed, too. (verse 34)

91. It was Jacob, and Isaac said he came deceitfully to take the blessing (verse 35)

92. Rebekah; it was her idea in the first place, and she told Jacob how to deceive his father. (in Genesis 27:5-17)

93. No; he was blind and didn't know he was being tricked.

94. Yes; in Genesis 25:29-34, Esau gave away his birthright (his right to inherit as the oldest son) for a bowl of stew. Note the end of verse 34: "So Esau despised his birthright." While this does not excuse the deceitful behavior of Rebekah or Jacob, it does implicate Esau, who didn't value his birthright until it was too late.

95. Esau meant that Jacob lived up to his name by deceiving his father in order to get the blessing from him.

96. He said he made Jacob lord over Esau, that he had made all his relatives Jacob's servants, and that he sustained him with grain and new wine. (verse 37)

97. He responded that Esau would live away from the earth's richness and from the dew of heaven, he would live by the sword and he would serve Jacob. Isaac added that Esau would eventually grow restless and throw off Jacob's authority over him. (verses 39-40)

Genesis 27:41-46

98. Esau held a grudge against Jacob. (verse 41)

99. Esau planned to kill his brother. (verse 41)

100. She told Jacob about Esau's plan to kill him, then told him to go at once to her brother Laban, and to stay there until Esau had calmed down. (verses 42-44)

101. She said she would send word for Jacob to come back. (verse 45)

102. She didn't want to lose both sons in one day: one to murder, and the other to being killed as punishment for being a murderer.

103. She said she sent Jacob away to find a wife so that he didn't marry one of the Hittite women from their own area. (verse 46)

104. Esau had married Hittite women.

Genesis 35: 27-29

105. Isaac lived to be 180 years old. (verse 28)

106. Esau and Jacob buried him. (verse 29)

107. No.

Short Essay Questions

1. Answers will vary.

2. Answers will vary.

3. Answers will vary.

4. Answers will vary, but should not ignore or dispute the fact that it was the Lord who told Rebekah that Esau would serve Jacob.

5. Answers will vary.

6. Isaac's blessing to Jacob (disguised as Esau): that God would give him rain and good crops, that people would serve him, and nations bow down to him, that he would be lord over his brothers, that his mother's son's would bow down to him, that God would curse those that cursed him and bless those that blessed him. God's blessing to

Rebekah

Abram: that He would make him a great nation, bless him, make his name great, he would be a blessing, bless those that bless him, curse those that curse him, all families of the earth blessed in him. The similarities are that both blessings request blessings on those who bless them and curses on those who curse them.

Rachel and Leah

Genesis 28:1-5

1. Isaac told Jacob to go to Paddan-aram. (verse 2)
2. Jacob was told to visit the house of his mother's father Bethuel. (verse 2)
3. Jacob was to choose a wife from among the daughters of his mother's brother Laban. (verse 2)
4. Isaac blessed Jacob, asking that God would bless him, make him fruitful and grow him into a community of people. He also asked that God would give Jacob and his descendants the same blessing given to Abraham, so they could take possession of the land that had been promised to Abraham. (verses 3-4)
5. Yes (verse 5)

Genesis 29:1-14

6. He saw a well with three flocks of sheep lying near it. (verse 1)
7. He asked them where they were from. (verse 4)
8. He asked them if they knew Laban. (verse 5)
9. They said, "Yes, we know him." (verse 5)
10. Their answer confirmed that he had come to the right place.
11. That Laban was well, and that his daughter Rachel was approaching with his sheep. (verse 6)
12. Rachel was a shepherdess for her father's sheep. (verse 9)
13. He rolled away the stone from the mouth of the well and watered the sheep for her. (verse 10)
14. Jacob kissed Rachel, wept aloud, and told Rachel he was a relative of her father and a son of Rebekah. (verses 11-12)
15. Rachel ran to tell her father about Jacob. (verse 12)
16. Laban was Jacob's mother's brother, i.e. Jacob's uncle. (verse 10)

17. Laban hugged and kissed Jacob, brought him to his home, and after hearing Jacob's story, told him, "Surely thou art my bone and my flesh." (verse 14)

Genesis 29:15-21

18. Laban asked Jacob what his wages should be. (verse 15)
19. Leah was the older sister and had weak eyes, while Rachel was younger and was beautiful. (verses 16-17)
20. Jacob said he would work for seven years in return for Rachel. (verse 18)
21. Jacob was in love with Rachel. (verse 18)
22. Yes (verse 19)
23. Jacob worked seven years for Rachel. (verse 20)
24. Quickly, because he was in love with Rachel. (verse 20)
25. Jacob had to ask Laban to give Rachel to him as his wife. (verse 21)

Genesis 29:22-30

26. Laban gave a feast (a wedding) for Jacob and his new wife. (verse 22)
27. Laban tricked Jacob by giving him Leah instead of Rachel as his wife. (verse 23)
28. Jacob felt deceived. (verse 25)
29. Laban said it was their custom that the older daughter had to be married first. (verse 26)
30. Laban told Jacob he could take Rachel as his wife after Leah's bridal week was over, as long as he worked seven more years for Laban. (verse 27)
31. Yes, he also married Rachel. (verse 28)
32. Jacob loved Rachel more than Leah. (verse 30)

Genesis 29:31-35

33. God opened Leah's womb, meaning He sent her a child. (verse 31)
34. Rachel was barren. (verse 31)
35. God sent Leah a baby boy, whom she named Reuben. (verse 32)
36. She said it was because God had seen her misery. (verse 32)
37. Leah thought Jacob would love her now that she had given him a son. (verse 32)

38. Leah had another son, whom she named Simeon. (verse 33)
39. She said God sent her Simeon because He had heard that she was hated. (verse 33)
40. Leah had a third son, whom she named Levi. (verse 34)
41. Leah said her husband would become attached to her because she had borne him three sons. (verse 34)
42. Leah gave birth to a son, whom she named Judah. (verse 35)
43. Leah said she would praise the Lord. (verse 35)
44. Leah stopped having children. (verse 35)

Genesis 30:1-8

45. Leah had four sons: Reuben, Simeon, Levi, and Judah.
46. Rachel had no children. (verse 1)
47. Rachel envied Leah. (verse 1)
48. She told Jacob, "Give me children, or I'll die!" (verse 1)
49. Jacob became angry with her and told her it was not him, but God, who had not given her children. (verse 2)
50. She gave her maidservant Bilhah to Jacob, and told him to sleep with her so she would have a child that would be part of Rachel's family. (verse 3)
51. Bilhah bore Jacob a son. (verse 5)
52. Rachel said God had vindicated her, by listening to her and giving her a son. Then she named the baby Dan. (verse 6)
53. Bilhah had another son by Jacob.
54. Rachel said she had a great struggle with her sister, and won. Then she named the baby Naphtali. (verse 8)

Genesis 30:9-13

55. Leah gave her maidservant Zilpah to Jacob as a wife. (verse 9)
56. Zilpah bore Jacob a son. (verse 10)
57. Leah said, "What good fortune!" and named the baby Gad. (verse 11)
58. Zilpah bore Jacob another son. (verse 12)
59. Leah was very happy, and named the baby Asher. (verse 13)

Rachel and Leah

Genesis 30:14-24

60. Reuben, Leah's eldest son, brought mandrake plants to Leah. (verse 14)

61. Rachel asked Leah to give her some of the plants. (verse 14)

62. Leah asked if it wasn't enough that Rachel had taken her husband, much less the mandrakes, too. (verse 15)

63. Rachel told Leah she would let Jacob sleep with Leah in exchange for the mandrakes. (verse 15)

64. Yes (verse 16)

65. Leah told Jacob she had hired him with her son's mandrakes, and that he had to sleep with her that night. (verse 16)

66. Leah became pregnant and bore Jacob a fifth son, because God listened to her. (verse 17)

67. In verse 18, Leah said God rewarded her.

68. No, she was jealous of Leah. (verse 1)

69. Leah bore Jacob a sixth son, whom she named Zebulun. (verses 19-20)

70. Leah said God gave her a precious gift. (verse 20)

71. Leah hoped it would make Jacob treat her with honor, because she had given him six sons. (verse 20)

72. Leah had a daughter, whom she named Dinah.

73. Leah had six sons and a daughter, plus the two sons her maidservant Zilpah had. Rachel had no children of her own, and the two sons her maidservant Bilhah had.

74. God remembered Rachel, listened to her and opened her womb, i.e. made her able to have children.

75. Rachel became pregnant and gave birth to a son, whom she named Joseph. (verse 24)

76. Rachel said, "The Lord shall add to me another son." (verse 24)

Genesis 31:14-21

77. They told Jacob to do what God had told him to do. (verse 16)

78. Jacob took his wives and children, his camels, his livestock, and all the goods he had accumulated in Paddan-aram. (verses 17-18)

79. Rachel stole her father's household images (gods). (verse 19)

80. Jacob didn't tell Laban he was going to run away. (verse 20)

Genesis 31:22-37

81. He took relatives with him, and pursued Jacob for seven days. (verse 23)
82. Laban caught up with Jacob. (verse 23)
83. God came to Laban in a dream. (verse 24)
84. Laban asked Jacob why he ran off secretly and deceived him, why he didn't let Laban give them a big send-off, why he didn't let him kiss his daughters and grandchildren good-bye, and why he stole his gods. (verses 26-30)
85. He was afraid Laban would take away his daughters (Jacob's wives) by force. (verse 31)
86. Jacob said that whoever had them would not live, and that Laban could search all through his belongings for them. (verse 32)
87. Jacob didn't know Rachel had stolen the gods. (verse 32)
88. No (verse 33)
89. No (verse 33)
90. No (verse 35)
91. Rachel was sitting on them. (verse 34)
92. Jacob became angry with Laban, and told him to show what, if anything, Laban had found that belonged to him among Jacob's possessions, so the assembled relatives could judge between the two of them. (verses 36-37)

Genesis 33:1-11

93. Jacob saw 400 men with Esau. (verse 1)
94. Jacob divided the children among the women. (verse 2)
95. Front row: Jacob
    Second row: the maidservants and their children
    Third row: Leah and her children
    Back row: Rachel and Joseph
96. Esau hugged and kissed Jacob, then they both wept. (verse 4)
97. He said they were "the children which God hath graciously given thy servant." (verse 5)
98. They bowed down to him. (verses 6-7)
99. He said he already had plenty, and that Jacob could keep all of it for himself. (verse 9)
100. He told Esau to please accept the gifts, because God had been gracious to him and he had all he needed. (verses 10-11)

Rachel and Leah

101. Esau accepted the gifts. (verse 11)

Genesis 35:16-20
102. Rachel began to give birth and had great difficulty. (verse 16)
103. The midwife told Rachel not to be afraid, and that she had another son. (verse 17)
104. Rachel named her son Ben-oni. (verse 18)
105. Jacob named the baby Benjamin. (verse 18)
106. Rachel died and was buried on the way to Ephrath. (verse 19)
107. Jacob put a pillar over Rachel's grave. (verse 20)

Genesis 48:7
108. He was sorrowful. (not in all translations)

Genesis 49:29-31
109. Leah was buried in the cave in the field of Ephron the Hittite, along with Jacob's parents and grandparents, and eventually Jacob himself. (verse 31)

Short Essay Questions
1. Answers will vary, but should include mention of the fact that Jacob's name meant *deceiver* and he had been deceptive in the past.
2. Answers will vary; Leah found comfort in her faith in God.
3. Neither wanted the disgrace of being barren, and worried what other women would say if they didn't have children. Also, being competitive with each other, each wanted to have more children than her sister, to the point of using handmaidens to increase the number of children considered theirs.
4. Answers will vary, but should include some of Rachel's traits: jealousy, competitive nature, lack of expressed gratitude to God for her first son, willingness to give Leah a night with Jacob in trade for some of her son's mandrakes, theft and lying.

5.

Birth Order	Name	Birth Mother
1	Reuben	Leah
2	Simeon	Leah
3	Levi	Leah
4	Judah	Leah
5	Dan	Bilhah (Rachel)
6	Naphtali	Bilhah (Rachel)
7	Gad	Zilpah (Leah)
8	Asher	Zilpah (Leah)
9	Issachar	Leah
10	Zebulun	Leah
11	Joseph	Rachel
12	Benjamin	Rachel

6. All verses indicate God's definition of marriage as one man and one woman. The Leviticus verse specifies that a man should not marry his wife's sister while his wife is living.

7. Answers will vary, but should mention that God says sex should be between one man and one woman within marriage. The fact that God allowed children to be born using Rachel and Leah's maidservants only indicates that God has His own purposes, not that He sent those children as a sign of approval of Rachel and Leah's purposes.

Rachel and Leah

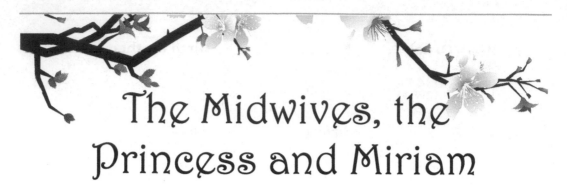

The Midwives, the Princess and Miriam

Exodus 1:1-22

1. The Israelites became exceedingly numerous, so that the land was filled with them. (verse 7)

2. He felt there were too many of them, and that if war broke out, they would side with the Egyptians' enemies. (verses 9-10)

3. They forced them into slavery. (verse 11)

4. The more they were oppressed, the more they multiplied and spread. (verse 12)

5. They worked them harder and ruthlessly. (verses 13-14)

6. Their names were Shiphrah and Puah. (verse 15)

7. A midwife is a woman who helps other women in childbirth.

8. The king of Egypt told them to kill the Hebrew boys at birth but let the girls live. (verse 16)

9. No; they let the baby boys live. (verse 17)

10. The midwives feared God, so they did not kill the baby boys of the Israelites. (verse 17)

11. The king asked them why they let the boys live. (verse 18)

12. They said the Hebrew women were so healthy they gave birth before they could get there. (verse 19)

13. He increased the Israelites further, and gave the midwives their own families. (verses 20-21)

14. He told them to throw every Hebrew baby boy into the river, but to let the girls live. (verse 22)

Exodus 2:1-10

15. The Levite woman hid her baby because he was a boy, and the Egyptians were murdering all of the Hebrew baby boys. (verse 2)
16. She hid him for three months. (verse 2)
17. She placed him in a waterproofed basket, which she hid in the reeds along the bank of the (Nile) River. (verse 3)
18. His sister stood watch over him. (verse 4)
19. Pharaoh's daughter, the princess, saw it when she came to the river to bathe. (verse 5)
20. The princess sent her maid to fetch the basket. (verse 5)
21. She felt sorry for the crying baby, which she knew was one of the Hebrew babies. (verse 6)
22. The baby's sister (verse 7)
23. She offered to find a Hebrew woman to nurse the baby. (verse 7)
24. Yes (verse 8)
25. The baby's mother (verse 8)
26. The Bible does not say.
27. She said she would pay the woman to nurse the baby. (verse 9)
28. His mother took him to the princess and he became her son. (verse 10)
29. She named him Moses. (verse 10)

Exodus 15:19-21

30. She is described as a prophetess and Aaron's sister. (verse 20)
31. A prophetess is a female prophet; a prophet is someone who is given instructions and a description of what will happen in the future by God.
32. Her father Amram, her mother Jochebed, and her brothers Moses and Aaron
33. She took a tambourine and sang to the women. (verse 20-21)
34. They followed Miriam, while shaking tambourines and dancing. (verse 20)
35. She said He had "triumphed gloriously," and that he hurled the Egyptians into the sea. (verse 21)
36. Yes (Micah 6:4)

The Midwives, the Princess and Miriam

Numbers 12:1-16

37. They began to talk against him because he had married a Cushite (a woman from the land of Cush, also called Ethiopia). (verse 1)

38. They asked whether God had only spoken through Moses, and not also through them. (verse 2)

39. God (verse 2)

40. He was more humble than anyone on earth. (verse 3)

41. He called Moses, Aaron and Miriam out to the tabernacle. (verse 4)

42. At once (verse 4)

43. In a pillar of cloud (verse 5)

44. God called Aaron and Miriam. (verse 5)

45. They stepped forward. (verse 5)

46. He reveals himself to a prophet in visions, and He speaks to him in dreams. (verse 6)

47. No (verse 7)

48. "Faithful"

49. He said He spoke to him "mouth to mouth....and not in dark speeches (riddles)." (verse 8)

50. God asked them why they were not afraid to speak against His servant Moses. (verse 8)

51. His anger burned against them, and He left them. (verse 9)

52. Miriam had been stricken with leprosy. (verse 10)

53. Leprosy is a disease that destroys the skin, leaving it white and ash-like.

54. Yes; he referred to "the sin we have.... done foolishly." (verse 11)

55. Aaron asked Moses not to hold their sin against them, so that Miriam would not end up severely stricken. (verses 11-12)

56. Moses cried out to God to heal Miriam. (verse 13)

57. God ordered that she be confined outside the camp for seven days, then she was brought back (cured of the leprosy) and the Israelites moved on. (verses 14-16)

Short Essay Questions

1. Answers will vary.
2. Moses' parents hid him because their faith in God led them to do so; that same faith gave them the courage to disobey the Pharaoh.
3. Answers will vary.
4. Answers will vary.
5. Answers will vary, but should mention that we, as the created, have no right to question our Creator, and that God is Holy.
6. Answers will vary, but should include that she was punished because she sinned, that God disciplines us because He loves us, and that parents discipline their children because they love them.

The Midwives, the Princess and Miriam

Rahab

Joshua 2:1-7

1. Two spies from Shittim (verse 1)
2. They stayed in the house of a prostitute named Rahab. (verse 1)
3. A prostitute is a woman who has sexual relations in exchange for money.
4. The king of Jericho (verse 2)
5. The king sent a message to Rahab. (verse 3)
6. He told Rahab to bring to him the men who were in her house, because they were spies. (verse 3)
7. She hid them.
8. She said the men had been at her house, but left, and she didn't know which way they had gone. (verses 4-5)
9. No
10. They were hidden under stalks of flax on Rahab's roof. (verse 6)
11. They left the city in pursuit of the spies. (verse 7)
12. Rahab had faith in God, which led her to help the Israelites.

Joshua 2:8-14

13. Rahab told the spies that she knew God had given Canaan to them. (verses 8-9)
14. The people of Jericho were terrified of the Israelites. (verses 9-11)
15. They had heard about how God helped the Israelites escape the Egyptians by parting the Red Sea, and how He helped them destroy Sihon and Og. (verse 10)
16. She asked them to give her a "true token" that they would spare her family from death when the Israelites attacked Jericho. (verses 12-13)
17. The spies promised her that they would protect her and her family, as long as she didn't tell anyone what they were up to. (verse 14)

Joshua 2:15-24

18. Rahab let the spies down by cord (rope) through a window of her house, which was built into the city wall, so they could escape. (verse 15)

19. She told them to go into the hills and hide for three days until the king's men had returned to Jericho. Then the spies could get away safely. (verse 16)

20. They said their promise to keep her family safe would only be binding if she tied a scarlet cord in the window after gathering all of her family in her house. (verses 17-18)

21. Anyone who left the house would be risking his own life, because the spies would only protect those in the house. (verse 19)

22. The spies would take the blame. (verse 19)

23. The spies would not have to stick to their promise to protect Rahab and her family. (verse 20)

24. Yes (verse 21)

25. She tied the scarlet cord in the window. (verse 21)

26. No (verse 22)

27. The spies told him the people of Jericho were afraid of the Israelites, and that God had certainly given the land to the Israelites. (verse 24)

Joshua 6:15-25

28. Joshua said that no one in the city would be spared except Rahab and her family. (verse 17)

29. He said Rahab and her family would be spared because she hid the spies sent by the Israelites. (verse 17)

30. They destroyed with the sword every person, cattle, sheep and donkey. (verse 21)

31. Joshua sent the spies to Rahab's house to rescue her and her family. (verse 23)

32. The spies took Rahab and her family to a place of safety outside the Israelites' camp. (verse 23)

33. It was completely burned down. (verse 24)

34. She continued to live among the Israelites.

Rahab

Matthew 1:5

35. Rahab married Salmon. (verse 5)
36. Their son's name was Boaz. (verse 5)
37. Jesus Christ

Short Essay Questions

1. Answers should include that marriage consists of one man and one woman who become one flesh (Genesis 2:24), that God creates children through sexual relations between man and wife (Genesis 4:1), that we are not to commit adultery (Exodus 20:14), that prostitution is wicked (Leviticus 19:29), that immorality has harsh consequences (Proverbs 5:1-14, Proverbs 6:20-35), that we are to glorify God with our bodies, not commit sin with them (1 Corinthians 6:15-20) and that Christians can live a holy life with the help of the Holy Spirit (1 Thessalonians 4:3-8).

2. Righteous is defined as "meeting the standards of what is right and just." Rahab's faith resulted in her righteous behavior. We are made righteous through faith in God.

3. Answers will vary.

4. Answers will vary.

Deborah and Jael

Judges 4:1-10

1. God saw them doing evil. (verse 1)
2. He sold them into the hands of Jabin, a king of Canaan. (verse 2)
3. Sisera was the commander of Jabin's army. (verse 2)
4. Sisera had been cruel and oppressive to the Israelites for 20 years. (verse 3)
5. They cried to Him for help. (verse 3)
6. A prophetess named Deborah was leading Israel at that time. (verse 4)
7. Deborah could be found holding court under the Palm of Deborah in the hill country of Ephraim, between Ramah and Bethel (verse 5)
8. She settled their disputes for them. (verse 5)
9. She sent for Barak, son of Abinoam from Kedesh in Naphtali. (verse 6)
10. Deborah told him to take 10,000 men and lead the way to Mount Tabor. (verse 6)
11. Deborah said she would lure Sisera, his chariots and his troops to the Kishon River, where he would be defeated by the Israelites. (verse 7)
12. He said he wouldn't go unless Deborah went with him. (verse 8)
13. Deborah said she would go with him, but because of his unwillingness to go without her, he would not have the honor of capturing Sisera. (verse 9)
14. Deborah said God would give that honor to a woman (verse 9)
15. They went to Kedesh. (verse 9)
16. Barak summoned the men of Zebulun and Naphtali. (verse 10)
17. Ten thousand men followed them. (verse 10)

Judges 4:11-18

18. He pitched his tent by the great tree in Zaanaim near Kedesh. (verse 11)
19. Sisera gathered together all of his men and his 900 chariots. (verses 12-13)
20. She sent him and his men off to fight against Sisera and his men. (verse 14)
21. God (verse 14)
22. Yes (verse 14)
23. Yes (verse 15)
24. God routed Sisera's army.
25. Sisera fled on foot, while his army was pursued by Barak and his men. (verses 15-16)
26. Sisera's men were slain by Barak's men. (verse 16)
27. Sisera ran to the tent of Heber the Kenite's wife Jael. (verse 17)
28. Sisera's king, Jabin, was friends with the clan of Heber the Kenite, so Sisera thought it was a safe place to hide. (verse 17)
29. Heber the Kenite's wife, Jael, invited him into her tent and hid him. (verse 18)

Judges 4:19-24

30. Sisera told Jael to give him some water. (verse 19)
31. Yes and no; she did give him a drink, but it was milk, not water. (verse 19)
32. Sisera told Jael to stand in the doorway and say "no" to anyone who might ask if someone was with her. (verse 20)
33. No (verse 21)
34. While Sisera was asleep, Jael took a hammer and used it to drive a tent peg through Sisera's temple. (verse 21)
35. He died. (verse 21)
36. Barak passed by while searching for Sisera. (verse 22)
37. Jael told Barak she could show him the man he was looking for. (verse 22)
38. Jael took Barak into the tent and showed him Sisera's body. (verse 22)
39. God subdued Jabin.
40. The Israelites "prospered, and prevailed against Jabin." (verse 24)

41. The Israelites destroyed him. (verse 24)

Judges 5

42. Mentions in Judges 5 about Deborah: village life ceased until she arose a mother in Israel (verse 7), God's people told her to wake up and sing (verse 12), the princes of Issachar were with her. (verse 15)

43. Mentions in Judges 5 about Jael: the era was described as "in the days of Jael" (verse 6), Jael was said to be the "most blessed of women" (verse 24), the wife of Heber the Kenite (verse 24), a tent-dwelling woman (verse 24), she gave Sisera curdled milk when he asked for water (verse 25), she pierced Sisera's temple and crushed his head. (verse 26)

44. Mentions in Judges 5 about God: He is the God of Israel (verse 3), God marched out from Seir and Edom (verse 4), mountains quaked before Him (verse 5), His acts are righteous (verse 11), His angel said to curse those who wouldn't help Him fight (verse 23), may His enemies die (verse 31), request for strength for those who love God. (verse 31)

45. There was peace there for forty years. (verse 31)

Short Essay Questions

1. Deborah was a prophetess and a judge, while Jael was the wife of a warrior. Deborah's position probably included servants and a nice home, while Jael, not having such a high position, lived in a tent. The fact that God used both of them to kill Sisera shows us that God uses all kinds of people (of both sexes), no matter what their social status, to do His will.

2. God rewards obedience and faith. Barak did not show either of those qualities when he refused to go after Sisera by himself, so God did not hand Sisera over to him. Instead, he handed Sisera over to a woman (as He had told Deborah He would), perhaps to shame him.

3. God could have given Jael strength to kill Sisera; he also could have put Sisera into a deep sleep so he didn't wake up when Jael drove the peg through his temple. God can do anything, which means we can ask for his help with seemingly impossible tasks, and if He wants them to happen, He'll make them happen.

Deborah and Jael

Ruth

Ruth 1:1-18

1. They went to Moab because there was a famine in their homeland of Judah. (verse 1)
2. The father was Elimelech, the mother was Naomi, and there were two sons named Mahlon and Chilion. (verse 2)
3. He died, leaving Naomi a widow. (verse 3)
4. Orpah and Ruth (verse 4)
5. Both sons died. (verse 5)
6. Naomi heard that there was now food in Judah. (verse 6)
7. God (verse 6)
8. Naomi made plans to return to her homeland. (verse 6)
9. Her daughters-in-law, Orpah and Ruth (verse 7)
10. Naomi told them to go back to their families, and that she hoped God would send them each another husband. (verses 8-9)
11. They cried and said they would go with her to her homeland. (verses 9-10)
12. Naomi said she would not be having more sons to become their husbands, and that she was too old to marry again. (verses 11-12)
13. She felt that "the hand of the Lord is gone out against me." (verse 13)
14. Orpah kissed Naomi good-bye, while Ruth held on to her. (verse 14)
15. Naomi said Orpah was going back to her family and her gods, and that Ruth should go with Orpah. (verse 19)
16. Ruth did not want to leave Naomi, and told her she wanted to stay with Naomi, and would not leave her until one of them died. (verses 16-18)
17. Naomi stopped telling Ruth to go back to Moab because she could see how strongly Ruth felt about going with her. (verse 18)

Ruth 1:19-22

18. They were the talk of the town; and many were surprised to see Naomi. (verse 19)
19. Naomi told the people to call her Mara (which means *bitter*), because she felt that God had made her life bitter by taking away her husband and sons. (verses 20-21)
20. It was the beginning of the barley harvest. (verse 22)

Ruth 2:1-9

21. His name was Boaz. (verse 1)
22. Ruth asked Naomi if she could pick up leftover grain in the fields. (verse 2)
23. Ruth gleaned in Boaz' field. (verse 3)
24. Boaz arrived. (verse 4)
25. Yes (verse 5)
26. The foreman told Boaz that Ruth had asked permission to glean in the field, and that she had worked hard all day with only a short break. (verses 6-7)
27. Boaz told Ruth to stay in his field instead of going to another field, and to stay with the girls. (verses 8-9)
28. Boaz had told the men not to touch her. (verse 9)
29. He told her to get a drink from the water jars whenever she was thirsty. (verse 9)

Ruth 2:10-17

30. She asked him why he was being so kind to her. (verse 10)
31. Boaz said he had heard about what Ruth had done for Naomi by coming with her to Bethlehem. He also told her he hoped God would bless her for her kindness to Naomi. (verses 11-12)
32. Boaz invited Ruth to have some bread with vinegar, and some roasted grain. (verse 14)
33. Boaz told the men not to embarrass Ruth while she gleaned, but to leave some extra stalks on the ground for her to find. (verses 15-16)
34. Ruth gathered about an ephah (29 lbs.) of barley. (verse 17)

Ruth

Ruth 2:18-23

35. She brought it to Naomi. (verse 18)
36. Naomi asked Ruth where she had gleaned that day. (verse 19)
37. Naomi said a blessing for him, then commented that he was still showing kindness, and also mentioned that he was a relative of theirs and one of their kinsman-redeemers. (verse 20)
38. Naomi told Ruth it would be better for her to stay with Boaz' girls, because she might be harmed in someone else's fields. (verse 22)
39. Yes, Ruth stayed close to Boaz' girls throughout the barley and wheat harvest. (verse 23)

Ruth 3:1-6

40. Naomi thought it was time for her to find a home for Ruth with another husband. (verse 1)
41. Boaz (verse 2)
42. Naomi told Ruth to wash and perfume herself and put on her best clothes before going to the threshing floor where Boaz would be. Then she was to wait until he was finished eating and drinking, and watch for him to lie down. Once he was lying on the floor, Ruth was to uncover his feet, lie down, and wait for Boaz to tell her what to do. (verses 3-4)
43. Yes, she did. (verse 6)

Ruth 3:7-15

44. Boaz lay down at the far end of the grain pile. (verse 7)
45. Ruth quietly uncovered his feet and lay down. (verse 7)
46. He discovered Ruth there in the middle of the night. (verse 8)
47. Ruth said she was his servant. (verse 9)
48. Ruth told Boaz to spread the corner of his garment over her because he was a kinsman-redeemer. Note: in that culture, Ruth's request was a way of asking Boaz to marry her and buy her husband's land. (verse 9)
49. He was pleased that she would ask him instead of someone richer or younger, and said he would do what she asked. (verses 10-11)
50. No; he said they knew of her noble character. (verse 11)
51. He did not because he knew of a relative closer than he, so he would have to notify that man of the situation and give him the first option to

marry Ruth. (verses 12-13)

52. Yes (verse 14)

53. Ruth left very early in the morning, while it was still dark enough that no one could see her. (verse 14)

54. Boaz poured six measures of barley into Ruth's shawl. (verse 15)

Ruth 3:16-18

55. Yes, she did. (verse 16)

56. Boaz told Ruth not to go back to her mother-in-law without food. (verse 17)

57. Naomi told Ruth to wait. (verse 18)

58. Yes, she thought he would settle the matter as soon as possible, even that day. (verse 18)

Ruth 4:1-12

59. Boaz went to the town gate. (verse 1)

60. "Then"; he did it even as Naomi and Ruth were discussing it. (verse 1)

61. He sat down when Boaz asked him to do so. (verse 1)

62. Ten of the town's elders (verse 2)

63. Boaz suggested that the kinsman-redeemer buy Elimilech's land since he had a right to do so, Boaz being in line behind him. (verses 3-4)

64. Yes, at first (verse 4)

65. Boaz said that buying the land meant the kinsman-redeemer would also be responsible for marrying Ruth. (verse 5)

66. He changed his mind and told Boaz to do it. (verse 6)

67. He said marrying Ruth might put his own estate in jeopardy. (verse 6)

68. He gave his sandal to Boaz. (verse 8)

69. It was how the Jewish people of that time legalized an agreement; today we would use a written contract. (verse 7)

70. He announced to the people that he was buying Naomi's family property, and that he would also marry Ruth. (verses 9-10)

71. Boaz said he would do this to keep Elimilech's family name with the property. (verse 10)

72. They acknowledged that they had witnessed the agreement. Then they asked for blessings for Boaz because he did this. (verses 11-12)

Ruth

73. Yes

74. That God would make Ruth like Rachel and Leah, whose sons were the forefathers of the Israelites, that Boaz would gain importance in Ephrathah and fame in Bethlehem for what he was doing, and that the family he would have with Ruth would be like that of his ancestor Perez.

Ruth 4:13-22

75. Boaz (verse 13)

76. Ruth gave birth to a son, who was from God. (verse 13)

77. They praised God for giving her a grandson, and hoped that he would someday find fame. (verse 14)

78. They said the baby would bring happiness to her life and take care of her in her old age. (verse 15)

79. They said she loved Naomi and had been kinder to her than seven sons. (verse 15)

80. Naomi held him in her lap and took care of him. (verse 16)

81. They named him Obed. (verse 17)

82. Obed's son was Jesse, and his grandson was David (the shepherd who killed Goliath, and the future king of Israel). (verse 17)

83. Perez, Hezron, Ram, Amminadab, Nahshon, Salmon, Boaz, Obed, Jesse, David (verses 18-22)

84. They were all ancestors of Jesus.

Short Essay Questions

1. Answers should include reference to the verses cited, which state that nothing happens that God does not know about, even a sparrow falling to the ground.

2. Verses refer to Ruth as being loving and loyal, hardworking, polite, obedient and kind.

3. Answers will vary.

4. Answers will vary, but should include references to God using all things for good for those that love Him, and He will restore lost years to us. God gave Naomi her daughter-in-law Ruth to care for her. He also used Ruth to give her a home and a grandson, rather than leave her bereft

and lonely after losing her husband and sons.

5.   Answers will vary.

6.   Answers will vary.

Hannah

1 Samuel 1:1-8

1. Elkanah had two wives, Hannah and Peninnah. (verse 2)

2. Yes, Peninnah had children. (verse 2)

3. No, Hannah did not have children. (verse 2)

4. Elkanah made a yearly trip to Shiloh to worship God and to offer sacrifices to Him. (verse 3)

5. The priests were Hophni and Phinehas. (verse 3)

6. His name was Eli. (verse 3)

7. He gave them all portions of meat. (verse 4)

8. He gave some to Peninnah and to her sons and daughters, and he gave a double portion to Hannah. (verse 5)

9. He gave Hannah a double portion because he loved her, and because God had closed her womb. (verse 5)

10. Peninnah teased Hannah about not having children, in order to make her fret. (verse 6)

11. Peninnah did it every year. (verse 7)

12. Hannah cried and refused to eat. (verse 7)

13. Elkanah asked her why she cried and refused to eat. He also asked her if he meant more to her than ten sons. (verse 8)

1 Samuel 1:9-18

14. Hannah stood up. (verse 9)

15. Eli the priest was sitting there. (verse 9)

16. She began to cry a lot and pray to God. (verse 10)

17. "Bitterness of soul" (verse 10)

18. She asked God to look at how sad she was and bless her with a son, and if He did this for her, she would give him back to God and his hair would never be cut (an indication that he would dedicate his life to

God). (verse 11)

19. Eli the priest was watching her. (verse 12)

20. He saw her lips moving but he couldn't hear any sound coming out. (verse 13)

21. He assumed she was drunk. (verse 13)

22. He told her to stop drinking, and to get rid of her wine. (verse 14)

23. She said she was very unhappy, so she was sharing her troubles with God. She also denied being wicked by getting drunk. (verses 15-16)

24. He told her to go in peace, and that God granted what she had been praying for. (verse 17)

25. She ate. (verse 18)

26. She was not upset anymore because she no longer looked sad. (verse 18)

1 Samuel 1:19-20

27. After worshipping God, they went back to their home in Ramah. (verse 19)

28. God remembered Hannah, and she became pregnant and had a son, whom she named Samuel. (verses 19-20)

29. It means *His name is God*, i.e. the God that heard Hannah when she asked Him for a son is the true God. (verse 20)

1 Samuel 1:21-28

30. Elkanah took his family to worship and make a sacrifice to God as he did every year. (verse 21)

31. Hannah and Samuel did not go with Elkanah. (verse 22)

32. Hannah said she would take Samuel there once he was weaned, and then he would stay there to live. (verse 22)

33. He said Hannah should do whatever she thought was best. (verse 23)

34. Hannah had promised God she would give Samuel to Him for His work. (verse 11)

35. Hannah took Samuel to the place of worship at Shiloh. (verse 24)

36. They took a three-year-old bull, flour and wine. (verse 24)

37. They would be offered as sacrifices to God. (see verses 3 and 21)

38. Samuel was brought to Eli the priest. (verse 25)

Hannah

39. Hannah told Eli that she was the woman who had prayed for a child there some time earlier, and that God had granted her request, so she was dedicating the child to the Lord. (verses 26-28)

1 Samuel 2:1-11

40. Hannah's prayer was one of joy and gratitude. (verse 1)
41. She said that God gives seven children to the barren woman. (verse 5)
42. In verse 6, she said that God "makes alive."
43. No; he remained with Eli the priest, where he "did minister unto the Lord." (verse 11)

1 Samuel 2:18-21

44. Samuel "ministered before the Lord." (verse 18)
45. He wore a linen ephod, or robe. (verse 18)
46. His mother made him a robe each year and brought it to Samuel when their family came to Shiloh for the annual sacrifice and worship. (verse 19)
47. He blessed them, asking that God would send them more children. (verse 20)
48. He sent her three sons and two daughters. (verse 21)

49. Samuel grew and found favor with God and with others.
50. Samuel became a prophet to whom God revealed Himself, and he shared God's messages with all the people of Israel.
51. Samuel was the judge (leader) of Israel.
52. Samuel remained the judge of Israel all his life.
53. When Samuel died, all of Israel mourned his death.
54. When Samuel called upon God, God answered him.
55. Samuel is listed among God's people of great faith.

Short Essay Questions

1.   Answers will vary. Bible verses indicate that those who love God don't slander people or say hurtful things to them on purpose, saying cruel things makes people unhappy, those who do not control what they say are ungodly, the tongue can cause great damage to others, and those who want a good life should watch their mouths.

2.   Hannah's trust that God would answer her prayer made her feel better. Bible verses indicate that we should wait on God to help us, trust Him to give us the desires of our hearts, our help only comes from God, our faith will be rewarded, and believe in God and Jesus instead of getting upset.

3.   Answers will vary.

4.   Answers will vary.

Hannah

Abigail

1 Samuel 25:1-3

1.   David moved down into the wilderness of Paran. (verse 1)
2.   His name was Nabal, and he was very wealthy and had property in Carmel. He had 1,000 goats and 3,000 sheep (which were being sheared in Carmel). Nabal was a Calebite, and was surly and mean. (verses 2-3)
3.   Her name was Abigail, and she was intelligent and beautiful. (verse 3)

1 Samuel 25:4-12

4.   David heard that Nabal was shearing sheep. (verse 4)
5.   David sent 10 young men to visit Nabal, to greet him in David's name, and to ask for some food. (verses 5-8)
6.   They were received rudely; Nabal refused to give them anything to eat. (verses 10-11)
7.   They returned to David and told him everything Nabal had said. (verse 12)

1 Samuel 25:13-17

8.   David told his men to put on their swords, and he put on his sword. (verse 13)
9.   He was known for killing tens of thousands of men in battle.
10. David was going to fight with Nabal.
11. About 400 men went with David. (verse 13)
12. There were 200 men who remained behind. (verse 13)
13. Some had to watch over their supplies. (verse 13)
14. He said Nabal hurled insults at David's men. (verse 14)
15. The servant said David's men had been very good to Nabal's servants, had not taken anything from them, and had even guarded them while

they were herding their sheep. (verses 15-16)

16. The servant knew David would be back to fight because Nabal had insulted him. (verse 17)

17. The servant knew Nabal wouldn't listen to him; he said Nabal was so wicked that no one could talk to him. (verse 17)

1 Samuel 25:18-22

18. Abigail "made haste." (verse 18)

19. She packed up 200 loaves of bread, two skins of wine, five dressed sheep, five measures of parched corn, 100 clusters of raisins, and 200 cakes of figs. (verse 18)

20. Abigail was bringing food to David's men, as he had originally requested.

21. Her servants were going with her. (verse 19)

22. No; she did not tell him. (verse 19)

23. Abigail met David and his men. (verse 20)

24. They intended to kill Nabal and his people. (verse 22)

1 Samuel 25:23-31

25. Abigail quickly got off her donkey and bowed before David. (verse 23)

26. Abigail fell at his feet and began to speak. (verse 24)

27. She took the blame. (verse 24)

28. She said he was wicked, that his name was Fool, and that folly went with him. (verse 25)

29. Abigail said she had not see them when they came and talked to Nabal. (verse 25)

30. She said the Lord had kept him from avenging himself. (verse 26)

31. She was giving the gift to David, and asked that he give it to his men. (verse 27)

32. Abigail requested blessings for David, therefore showing him that she respected him. She did this to soften David's heart in hopes he would decide against punishing Nabal and his household.

33. Abigail told David that once God made him leader over Israel, David wouldn't want the guilt of knowing that he killed Nabal's family in revenge. (verse 30)

Abigail

34. She asked that he remember her once God brought him success. (verse 31)

1 Samuel 25:32-35

35. David said God had sent Abigail. (verse 32)

36. He said Abigail should be blessed for (1) having good judgment and (2) for keeping himself from murdering out of revenge. (verse 33)

37. David said none of the men belonging to Nabal would have been alive by the next morning. (verse 34)

38. Yes (verse 35)

39. He told her to go home in peace. (verse 35)

40. He said he had heard her words and granted her request. (verse 35)

1 Samuel 25:36-42

41. Nabal was holding a banquet as a king would have done. (verse 36)

42. He was happy and drunk. (verse 36)

43. She didn't tell him anything until the morning. (verse 36)

44. Abigail told him what had happened with David. (verse 37)

45. Nabal had heart failure and went into shock. (verse 37)

46. No (verse 38)

47. God struck him down and he died. (verse 38)

48. David said God brought about Nabal's death. (verse 39)

49. He said God punished Nabal for his wrongdoing. (verse 39)

50. David said God had kept him from doing wrong. (verse 39)

51. David asked Abigail to marry him. (verse 39)

52. He sent his servants to see her at Carmel and ask her. (verse 40)

53. Yes (verse 41)

54. Abigail quickly went to David to marry him. (verse 42)

55. No, she took her five maids with her. (verse 42)

56. When David fled Saul by escaping to the land of the Philistines, he took Abigail with him.

57. The Amalekites took Abigail and the rest of the families of David and his men captive, but they were later rescued unharmed.

58. David took Abigail and his other wife Ahinoam to Hebron to live.
59. Abigail and David had a son named Chiliab or Kiliab (also called Daniel); see 1 Chronicles 3:1.

Short Essay Questions

1. Abigail quickly reacted to prevent a tragedy, she didn't tell her husband that she was sending food to David and his men, she humbled herself before David, she apologized for her husband's behavior, she asked for forgiveness on behalf of her husband, she made David realize that killing Nabal and his family would not be a good thing for him personally, she waited to tell Nabal about what happened until he was sober, and she accepted David's proposal of marriage.

2. Answers will vary.

3. Bible verses indicate God may humble us at times to test us or teach us, we are to humble ourselves before God, those who humble themselves will be honored and exalted, we should humble ourselves like a child, like Jesus who humbled himself by coming to earth and dying on a cross for us, God gives grace to the humble, and we should act with humility toward each other.

Abigail

Bathsheba

2 Samuel 3:2-5

1. Their names were Ahinoam, Abigail, Maacah, Haggith, Abital and Eglah. (verses 3-5)
2. Her name was Michal.
3. David took more concubines and wives.
4. No, it did not.

2 Samuel 11:1-5

5. "The time when kings go forth to battle." (verse 1)
6. No (verse 1)
7. He sent Joab out with the entire army. (verse 1)
8. They wiped out the Ammonites and put the city of Rabbah under siege. (verse 1)
9. King David stayed in Jerusalem. (verse 1)
10. He got up and went for a walk on the palace roof. (verse 2)
11. He saw a beautiful woman bathing. (verse 2)
12. He sent a man to find out who she was. (verse 3)
13. David learned that the woman's name was Bathsheba, and that she was the daughter of Eliam and the wife of Uriah the Hittite. (verse 3)
14. David sent messengers to get her. (verse 4)
15. David and Bathsheba slept together, then she went back to her house. (verse 4)
16. Bathsheba sent a message to David letting him know that she was pregnant. (verse 5)

2 Samuel 11:6-13

17. David sent for Uriah the Hittite. (verse 6)
18. Uriah the Hittite, in response to David's order (verse 7)

19. David told Uriah to go home and wash his feet. (verse 8)

20. David sent Uriah a gift of meat. (verse 8)

21. No, he didn't go home, but instead slept at the palace entrance with David's servants. (verse 9)

22. David asked Uriah why he didn't go home to sleep. (verse 10)

23. He didn't feel right going home to his wife when his fellow soldiers were out at battle. (verse 11)

24. David invited Uriah to eat and drink with him. (verse 13)

25. David got Uriah drunk. (verse 13)

26. No; he again slept where the king's servants slept. (verse 13)

2 Samuel 11:14-25

27. David sent Uriah back into battle. (verse 14)

28. David told Joab to put Uriah into the front line, the most dangerous area, and to then leave him unprotected so he would be killed. (verse 15)

29. Yes (verse 16)

30. He was killed by the enemy soldiers. (verse 17)

31. Joab expected David to be angry. (verses 19-21)

32. He told him to tell David that "Thy servant Uriah the Hittite is dead also." (verse 21)

33. He told the messenger to encourage Joab. (verse 25)

34. No (verse 25)

2 Samuel 11:26-27

35. Bathsheba is referred to as 'the wife of Uriah.'

36. She mourned for her husband. (verse 26)

37. David brought her to the palace. (verse 27)

38. They were married and Bathsheba had a baby boy. (verse 27)

39. God was displeased. (verse 27)

2 Samuel 12:1 and 7-14

40. God sent Nathan to talk to David. (verse 1)

41. In verse 9, Nathan said, "Thou hast killed Uriah the Hittite with the sword, and hast taken his wife to be thy wife, and hast slain him with

the sword of the children of Ammon."

42. He said, "...the sword shall never depart from thine house." (verse 10)

43. David admitted he had sinned. (verse 13)

44. Nathan said God had taken away David's sin, and that David was not going to die. (verse 13)

45. He said David's son would die. (verse 14)

2 Samuel 12:15-24

46. He became sick. (verse 15)

47. God caused the child to become sick. (verse 15)

48. David pleaded with God, fasted and lay on the ground all night. (verses 16-17)

49. He died. (verse 18)

50. They were afraid of his reaction. (verse 18)

51. David washed, changed clothes, went to worship God, and ate food. (verse 20)

52. Before his son died, David hoped God would change his mind and spare the child, so he pleaded for his life. But once the boy died, David knew he couldn't bring the boy back again. (verses 22-23)

53. In verse 24, David comforted Bathsheba, so we know she was upset.

54. He sent them a son, whom they named Solomon. (verse 24)

1 Chronicles 3:5

55. Bathsheba was blessed with four sons. (verse 5)

56. Bathsheba's children were Shimea, Shobab, Nathan and Solomon. (verse 5)

1 Kings 1:11-27

57. He told her that Adonijah, one of David's other sons, had proclaimed himself king without David's knowledge. (verse 11)

58. Nathan suggested to Bathsheba that she go to David and remind him that he had said that Solomon would be king, and then ask why Adonijah was king instead. (verses 12-13)

59. He would come in to see David and confirm what Bathsheba had said. (verse 14)

60. She reminded him that Solomon was supposed to be the king after David, then added that Adonijah had claimed the position, and celebrated it without even inviting Solomon. She also urged him to make a public statement identifying the new king. (verses 17-20)
61. Bathsheba said she was afraid that as soon as David died, she and her son Solomon would be treated like criminals if Adonijah was king. (verse 21)
62. Yes, he came in to see David and confirmed what Bathsheba had said. (verses 22-26)
63. Nathan asked David if it was his idea for Adonijah to be king. (verse 27)

1 Kings 1:28-35

64. King David called for his wife Bathsheba. (verse 28)
65. He told her that he would make Solomon the king. (verse 30)
66. She bowed before him, then knelt and said "Let my lord King David live forever." (verse 31)
67. He told them to anoint Solomon as king of Israel. (verse 34)

1 Kings 1:39-53

68. Yes, they anointed Solomon as king. (verse 39)
69. He grabbed the horns of the altar because he was afraid that Solomon would have him killed. (verses 50-51)
70. No; he said if he could be good, he would live. Then he sent him home. (verses 52-53)

1 Kings 2:10-20

71. He had been king for forty years. (verse 11)
72. "Established greatly" (verse 12)
73. He asked her to ask the king to give him Abishag the Shunammite as his wife. (verse 17)
74. He knew the king would not refuse a request from her. (verse 17)
75. Yes, she agreed. (verse 18)
76. He stood up, bowed to her and sat on his throne. Then he sent for another throne for her to sit on, and had it placed at his right hand. (verse 19)

Bathsheba

77. Before he even knew what the request was, the king said he would not refuse her. (verse 20)

78. Solomon (in Matthew 1:6) and Nathan (in Luke 3:31)

Short Essay Questions

1. The temptation came from Satan. The remainder of the answer will vary.

2. The phrase referring to Bathsheba is "wife of Uriah" or "Uriah's wife." Bathsheba is not referred to as David's wife until after their son has died (i.e. after David's punishment was over).

3. Answers will vary, but the verses point to David being the wrongdoer in this situation.

4. Answers will vary.

5. Answers will vary.

The Shunammite Woman

2 Kings 4:8-17

1. Elisha went to Shunem. (verse 8)
2. She was "great," meaning wealthy. (verse 8)
3. She offered him a meal. (verse 8)
4. He ate at her house whenever he was nearby. (verse 8)
5. She said she knew that Elisha was "a holy man of God." (verse 9)
6. She made a guest room for Elisha on the roof of her house. (verse 10)
7. He was grateful and wanted to do something for her. (verses 11-13)
8. Elisha's servant Gehazi (verse 12)
9. He asked her if there was anything he could do for her, since she had done so much to help him out. (verse 13)
10. No (verse 13)
11. Gehazi pointed out that she had no son, and that her husband was elderly. (verse 14)
12. He said she would have a son within the year. (verse 16)
13. She told him not to lie to her. (verse 16)
14. Yes; she became pregnant, and had a son about a year later. (verse 17)

2 Kings 4:18-25

15. He complained that his head hurt. (verses 18-19)
16. He told his servant to carry the boy to his mother. (verse 19)
17. The boy died in his mother's lap. (verse 20)
18. The Shunammite woman laid the boy on Elisha's bed, then shut the door and left. (verse 21)
19. She asked him to send for a servant and a donkey so she could go see Elisha and come right back. (verse 22)

20. No

21. She said, "It shall be well." (verse 23)

22. No, she told the servant not to slow down unless she ordered him to do so. (verse 24)

23. Yes, at Mount Carmel (verse 25)

2 Kings 4: 26-37

24. He told Gehazi to run to meet her. (verses 25-26)

25. Elisha wanted to know if she and her family were well. (verse 26)

26. She grabbed his feet. (verse 27)

27. He moved to push her away. (verse 27)

28. Elisha said to leave her alone, that she was very upset but that God had not told him why she was upset. (verse 27)

29. She asked Elisha whether she had asked for a son, and reminded him that she had told him not to deceive her. (verse 28)

30. He told Gehazi to run directly to the boy and lay his (Elisha's) staff on his face. (verse 29)

31. Yes (verse 30)

32. Yes (verse 30)

33. He did not react at all. (verse 31)

34. Elisha shut the door, prayed to God, and then stretched out over the boy until the boy's body grew warm. (verses 33-34)

35. He stretched over the boy one more time. (verse 35)

36. He sneezed seven times, then opened his eyes. (verse 35)

37. Elisha told Gehazi to call the Shunammite woman. (verse 36)

38. The Shunammite woman fell at Elisha's feet and bowed low, then took her son and left the room. (verse 37)

2 Kings 8:1-6

39. Elisha told the Shunammite woman to leave the area with her family. (verse 1)

40. He said God had decreed a famine for the area, and that it would last seven years. (verse 1)

41. Yes, she and her family went away. (verse 2)

42. They went to the land of the Philistines. (verse 2)

43. They lived there for seven years. (verse 2)
44. They came back to their homeland. (verse 3)
45. She went to see the king. (verse 3)
46. She went to beg the king for the return of her house and land. (verse 3)
47. He was talking with Gehazi, Elisha's servant. (verse 4)
48. The king asked Gehazi to tell him about all the wonderful things Elisha had done. (verse 4)
49. Gehazi was telling the king about how Elisha had brought the Shunammite's son back to life after he died. (verse 5)
50. Gehazi introduced her as the woman whose son Elisha restored to life. (verse 5)
51. He asked the Shunammite woman about what happened to her son. (verse 6)
52. She told him about it. (verse 6)
53. He helped her to get back everything that belonged to her, plus the income that her land had generated while she was away. (verse 6)

Short Essay Questions

1. She believed that Elisha had power from God, and that once she told him what had happened, God could use him to bring her son back to life. That's why she kept insisting everything "shall be well."
2. Both women gave the prophets food, both prophets performed miracles that helped the women, both women's sons died, both women told the prophets about their sons' deaths, both boys were taken to the prophets' rooms, and both prophets stretched out over the dead boys and breathed life back into them through the power of God.
3. Answers will vary, but should relate to the fact that Elisha's previous prophecy had been accurate.
4. Answers will vary.

The Shunammite Woman

Jezebel

1 Kings 16:29-31

1. Ahab (verse 29)

2. He would reign for 22 years. (verse 29)

3. He did more evil in the eyes of God than any of the kings who ruled before him. (verse 30)

4. Ahab married Jezebel and began to serve and worship the false god Baal. (verse 31)

1 Kings 18:1-4

5. God told Elijah to go to see King Ahab, after which God would send rain to relieve the drought the country had suffered. (verse 1)

6. Yes, he went to see Ahab. (verse 2)

7. Yes, it was a severe famine. (verse 2)

8. Ahab summoned Obadiah. (verse 3)

9. Obadiah ran Ahab's palace. (verse 3)

10. Obadiah "feared the Lord greatly," i.e. had a strong faith in God. (verse 3)

11. She had been murdering God's prophets. (verse 4)

12. Obadiah had hidden 50 prophets each in two caves and provided them with food and water. (verse 4)

1 Kings 19:1-3

13. Ahab told his wife Jezebel about what Elijah had done to their prophets. (verse 1)

14. Jezebel sent a message to Elijah, telling him she would make sure he was dead by the very next day. (verse 2)

15. Elijah ran for his life. (verse 3)

1 Kings 21:1-16

16. Ahab asked Naboth to either trade vineyards with him, or let him buy his vineyard. (verse 2)

17. He refused, not wanting to give up something left to him by his ancestors. (verse 3)

18. Ahab pouted on his bed and refused to eat. (verse 4)

19. She commented on his behavior (considering he was the king, after all), then told him to eat, and to cheer up because she was going to get him the vineyard. (verse 7)

20. Jezebel arranged for Naboth to be accused of something he didn't do and to be punished by being stoned to death. (verses 8-10)

21. The elders and nobles of Naboth's city helped in the plot against Naboth. (verses 8-13)

22. The people who murdered him. (verse 14)

23. Jezebel told Ahab to take possession of Naboth's vineyard because he had died. (verse 15)

24. Yes; he took over Naboth's vineyard. (verse 16)

1 Kings 21:17-29

25. God told Elijah to meet with Ahab. (verse 18)

26. God said Ahab was in Naboth's vineyard, which he took for himself. (verse 18)

27. God told Elijah to tell Ahab that 1) God knew he murdered Naboth and stole his vineyard, and 2) that Ahab would die (the dogs would lick up his blood) just as Naboth did. (verse 19)

28. Ahab referred to Elijah as his enemy. (verse 20)

29. Elijah said he would bring disaster on Ahab, kill his descendants, separate Ahab from every male in Israel, and make his house (family line) like those of Jeroboam and Baasha. (verses 21-22)

30. He said it was because Ahab had made him angry, and had also caused Israel to sin. (verse 22)

31. Elijah said that dogs would eat her by the wall of Jezreel. (verse 23)

32. Ahab sinned against God and worshipped idols. Jezebel encouraged him to sin. (verse 25)

33. Ahab became very remorseful and mourned by tearing his clothes,

Jezebel

putting on sackcloth and fasting. (verse 27)

34. God said because of Ahab's willingness to humble himself in reaction to Elijah's words about his behavior, God would postpone the punishment of Ahab's family until after Ahab was gone and his son was in charge. (verses 28-29)

2 Kings 9:6-10

35. Elisha told Jehu that God wanted him to destroy Ahab's house (descendants). (verse 7)

36. God wanted to avenge the deaths of his prophets and servants, which had been ordered by Jezebel (1 Kings 18:4). (verse 7)

37. No; he said the whole house would die. (verse 8)

38. Elisha said that dogs would devour her at Jezreel, and that no one would bury her. (verse 10)

2 Kings 9:30-37

39. Jezebel put on makeup, fixed her hair, and watched for him through a window. (verse 30)

40. She referred to him as the murderer of his master. (verse 31)

41. He asked who was on his side. (verse 32)

42. Jehu told the servants to throw her down, so they threw her out of the window. (verses 32-33)

43. It was trampled by horses. (verse 33)

44. Jehu ate and drank, and told the servants to bury Jezebel because she was the daughter of a king. (verse 34)

45. All that was left of her was her skull, hands and feet. (verse 35)

46. Elijah had said that Jezebel would be devoured by dogs. (verses 36-37)

Short Essay Questions

1. Answers will vary. Bible verses indicate God knows what we need, that everything (including not getting something we wanted) works for good for those that love God, being envious does not come from God, and our requests are sometimes refused because we don't have God-pleasing motives.

2. Yes, she was guilty of murder, and also of using her position to force others to commit sins, because what she did was against God's word, and in the case of murdering the prophets, in purposeful opposition to God.

3. See Proverbs 31:10-31.

Esther

Esther 1:1-9

1. Ahasuerus, also known by his Greek name, Xerxes. (verse 1)
2. King Xerxes was the ruler of 127 provinces, from India to Ethiopia. (verse 1)
3. King Xerxes lived and ruled in the citadel of Susa. (verse 2)
4. He held a royal banquet for the important people in his kingdom. (verse 3)
5. The king displayed all of his wealth. (verse 4)
6. He displayed it for 180 days. (verse 4)
7. The banquet was seven days long. (verse 5)
8. There were white, green and blue linen hangings tied with white and purple cords hanging from marble pillars by silver rings, and gold and silver couches on jeweled mosaic pavement. (verse 6)
9. The wine was plentiful, and served in unique gold goblets. Guests were free to drink as much as they wanted. (verses 7-8)
10. The king's wife, Queen Vashti, held a banquet in the palace for the women. (verse 9)

Esther 1:10-22

11. He was tipsy, and possibly drunk. (verse 10)
12. The king commanded his seven eunuchs (Mehuman, Biztha, Harbona, Bigtha, Abagtha, Zethar and Carcas) to bring Queen Vashti to him, and she should be wearing her royal crown. (verses 10-11)
13. The king wanted to show off the queen's beauty to his guests. (verse 11)
14. The eunuchs obeyed him, but Queen Vashti refused to come. (verse 12)
15. Yes; he became very angry. (verse 12)
16. He asked his experts (Carshena, Shethar, Admatha, Tarshish, Meres, Marsena and Memucan) what should be done to Queen Vashti in light

of her disobedience. (verses 13-15)

17. The experts told him that the queen had wronged the king and his people by disobeying him. (verse 16)

18. The experts said that the women of the land would disobey their husbands and other authorities because of the queen's example of disobedience. (verses 17-18)

19. The experts thought the king should decree that Queen Vashti could not be in his presence, and he should then find a new queen to replace her. (verse 19)

20. They believed that when the women of the land heard what happened to Queen Vashti, they would obey their husbands. (verse 20)

21. King Xerxes and his nobles liked this advice, and sent out a decree to every province declaring that men were to be the rulers of their households. (verse 22)

Esther 2:1-4

22. He remembered those things after his anger had subsided. (verse 1)

23. His attendants suggested that he search for beautiful young virgin women and bring them into his harem. (verses 2-3)

24. The young women would be cared for by Hegai, the king's eunuch, and given beauty treatments. (verse 3)

25. Whichever girl pleased King Xerxes would replace Vashti as queen. (verse 4)

26. He liked the idea, and decided to do as they suggested. (verse 4)

Esther 2:5-11

27. Mordecai had been brought there as a captive from Jerusalem. (verses 5-6)

28. His cousin's name was Hadassah (also called Esther). Mordecai took her in as his daughter when her parents died. (verse 7)

29. "Fair and beautiful" (verse 7)

30. Esther was taken to the palace as part of the harem. (verse 8)

31. He liked her a lot; she made a good impression on him. (verse 9)

32. Hegai gave Esther special food and beauty treatments, seven maids from the palace and the best place in the harem. (verse 9)

Esther

33. No one there knew that Esther was a Jew because Mordecai had told her not to tell anyone. (verse 10)

34. Mordecai checked on Esther daily by pacing the courtyard of the harem in search of news about her. (verse 11)

Esther 2:12-18

35. The girls had to have a year's worth of beauty treatments: six months using oil of myrrh and six months using perfumes and cosmetics. (verse 12)

36. She could take anything she wanted. (verse 13)

37. When it was a girl's turn to visit the king, she went there in the evening and returned to the harem the next morning. (verse 14)

38. If the king was pleased with a girl, he would summon her by name. (verse 14)

39. She only asked to bring the things that Hegai (the eunuch) suggested that she bring. (verse 15)

40. They all liked her. (verse 15)

41. Esther visited the king during Tebeth, the tenth month, during the seventh year of the king's reign. (verse 16)

42. He loved her better than any of the other girls. (verse 17)

43. The king put a crown on her head, and made her the new queen. (verse 17)

44. The king held a banquet in honor of Esther, declared a tax holiday everywhere he reigned, and gave everyone presents. (verse 18)

Esther 2:19-23

45. Mordecai (verse 19)

46. No; she had kept it a secret. (verse 20)

47. She did not tell anyone about her family or her heritage. (verse 20)

48. He overheard two guards plotting to kill King Xerxes. (verse 21)

49. He told Esther about the plot, and she told the king, making sure to mention that it was Mordecai who told her first. (verse 22)

50. Once it was determined that Mordecai was right, the two guards were hanged. (verse 23)

51. No

52. This event was written down in the king's book while he watched. (verse 23)

Esther 3:1-15

53. Haman (verse 1)
54. It doesn't say why he was honored.
55. He placed him in a seat of honor that was higher than the seats of the other nobles. (verse 1)
56. They bowed down in front of Haman and paid honor to him. (verse 2)
57. The king had commanded them to do it for Haman. (verse 2)
58. Mordecai refused. (verse 2)
59. He would not say why. (verses 3-4)
60. They told Haman about it. (verse 4)
61. They wanted to see if Mordecai would get away with it, because they knew he was a Jew. (verse 4)
62. Haman was furious. (verse 5)
63. Haman wanted to punish not just Mordecai, but all the Jews. (verse 6)
64. It was a lot that they would cast when making a decision. (verse 7)
65. Haman told King Xerxes that there was a group of people in his kingdom who did not obey the king's laws, and that he wanted the king to decree that they be put to death. (verses 8-9)
66. Haman suggested giving them 10,000 talents of silver. (verse 9)
67. The king gave Haman his ring, told him to keep the money and that he could do whatever he wished with the group of people he had mentioned. (verse 10)
68. With the king's permission, Haman ordered that all Jews be killed on the thirteenth day of Adar, and their wealth confiscated. (verses 12-13)
69. Every province ruled by King Xerxes received this decree. (verse 14)
70. King Xerxes ruled 127 provinces. (Esther 1:1)
71. They were sealed with the king's ring, which he had given to Haman. (verse 12)
72. They were sent out so that all of the king's subjects would be ready to kill the Jews on the thirteenth day of Adar. (verse 14)
73. They were perplexed. (verse 15)

Esther

Esther 4:1-11

74. Mordecai tore his clothes, changed into sackcloth and ashes, and publicly mourned the edict. (verse 1)

75. He stopped at the king's gate; he couldn't go farther because he was dressed in sackcloth, which was not allowed there. (verse 2)

76. They also mourned as Mordecai did. (verse 3)

77. Esther's maids and eunuchs told her what Mordecai was doing. (verse 4)

78. She sent regular clothes to him. (verse 4)

79. No, he refused to change out of the sackcloth (mourning clothes). (verse 4)

80. No (verse 5)

81. Esther sent Hathach the eunuch to find out why Mordecai was upset. (verse 5)

82. Mordecai told the eunuch how much money Haman was going to pay for the death of the Jews, gave him a copy of the edict for Esther to see, and told him to urge Esther to go to the king with this information. (verses 7-8)

83. The eunuch went back to Esther, and shared everything from Mordecai with her. (verse 9)

84. She told the eunuch to tell Mordecai that according to the law, anyone who approached the king without permission faced death, unless the king extended his gold scepter to spare the person's life. She added that she had not been summoned to see the king for thirty days. (verses 10-11)

Esther 4:12-17

85. Mordecai told Esther not to think she would be spared just because she was in the king's house. (verse 13)

86. Mordecai said that help for the Jews would arrive from somewhere else, but that she and her family would not survive. (verse 14)

87. He suggested that saving her people might be the reason she was chosen to live in the king's palace. (verse 14)

88. Esther sent word to Mordecai to have all the Jews in Susa fast for her for three days. (verses 15-16)

89. Esther and her maids would also fast for three days. (verse 16)
90. Esther would go to the king. (verse 16)
91. Esther said she knew that going to the king was against the law, and she understood she could be killed for it. (verse 16)
92. Yes (verse 17)

Esther 5:1-8

93. Esther put on her royal robes. (verse 1)
94. The king held out the gold scepter to her. (verse 2)
95. Esther walked toward the king and touched the end of the scepter. (verse 2)
96. The king said she could request up to half of his kingdom. (verse 3)
97. Esther invited him to a banquet she had prepared for him and Haman. (verse 4)
98. He summoned Haman so they could go to Esther's banquet right away. (verse 5)
99. Yes, he and Haman attended Esther's banquet. (verse 5)
100. The king asked Esther what she wanted to request of him, and reminded her that she could have up to half of the kingdom. (verse 6)
101. Esther asked if the king and Haman would come to another banquet she would prepare for them the next day, where she would tell the king what she was asking of him. (verses 7-8)

Esther 5:9-14

102. Haman left the banquet in a very good mood. (verse 9)
103. Haman saw Mordecai, and noticed that Mordecai did not act respectfully or fearfully around him, and that enraged him. (verse 9)
104. No; he kept himself from responding to Mordecai's slight and went home. (verse 10)
105. He gathered together his wife and friends so he could brag about how wealthy he was, how many sons he had and how the king had honored him in the past. (verses 10-11)
106. Haman bragged about being invited to dine alone with the king and queen, and about how he was invited back again the next day for another banquet. (verse 12)

Esther

107. Haman said seeing Mordecai the Jew sitting at the king's gate took away his satisfaction. (verse 13)

108. They suggested he build a gallows 50 cubits (75 feet) high and ask the king to use it to hang Mordecai, and then go to the banquet with the king. (verse 14)

109. Yes; he had a gallows built for Mordecai. (verse 14)

Esther 6:1-10

110. The king had trouble getting to sleep. (verse 1)

111. He sent for the record of his reign to be read to him. (verse 1)

112. He learned that Mordecai had saved his life by reporting an assassination conspiracy plotted by two of his guards. (verse 2)

113. The king asked his attendants if Mordecai had been rewarded for saving the king's life. (verse 3)

114. They told the king that Mordecai had not been rewarded. (verse 3)

115. The king asked his attendants who was in the court. (verse 4)

116. Haman was in the court, waiting to ask the king if he could have Mordecai hanged on the gallows he had just erected for that purpose. (verse 4)

117. They told the king that Haman was in the court. (verse 5)

118. The king told the attendants to bring Haman in to see him. (verse 5)

119. The king asked Haman how he should treat someone he wanted to honor. (verse 6)

120. Haman thought the king intended to honor him. (verse 6)

121. Haman told the king he should honor that man by giving him one of his royal robes to wear and a royal horse (wearing a royal crown on its head) to ride, and that he should then have the man taken through the city on the horse while it is proclaimed that the king wants to honor the man. (verses 7-9)

122. Yes (verse 10)

123. The king ordered Haman to honor Mordecai in just the way Haman had suggested. (verse 10)

124. No; he told him not to leave any of it out. (verse 10)

Esther 6:11-14

125. Yes (verse 11)

126. Haman had to get the royal robe and horse, put the robe on Mordecai, and lead him (seated on the horse) around the town while proclaiming that Mordecai was the man the king wanted to honor. (verse 11)

127. Haman rushed home and told his wife and friends what had happened. The Bible says his head was covered in grief. (verses 12-13)

128. They told him that he would fall before Mordecai because Mordecai was Jewish. (verse 13)

129. The king's eunuchs came and took Haman away to Esther's banquet. (verse 14)

Esther 7:1-10

130. The king and Haman attended Esther's banquet. (verse 1)

131. The king asked her what her petition was. (verse 2)

132. The king told Esther that he would grant her petition, and then reminded her that she could ask for up to half of his kingdom. (verse 2)

133. Esther asked the king to spare her life and the lives of her people. (verse 3)

134. Esther told the king that someone planned to exterminate her race. (verse 4)

135. Esther said she would not have bothered the king if her people had been sold into slavery. (verse 4)

136. The king wanted to know who would dare to kill Esther and her people. (verse 5)

137. Esther told the king that Haman was responsible. She described Haman as wicked, and an enemy and adversary. (verse 6)

138. Haman was afraid. (verse 6)

139. The king was so angry that he went outside, to the garden. (verse 7)

140. Haman decided that since the king was angry with him, he would try to get Esther to spare him from being punished by the king. (verse 7)

141. Haman, begging Esther for his life, fell on the couch where she reclined. (verse 8)

142. He accused Haman of attacking Esther. (verse 8)

Esther

143. His head was covered. (verse 8)
144. He mentioned that Haman had built a gallows by his house, intending it for Mordecai. (verse 9)
145. He was hung on the gallows by his house. (verse 10)
146. His anger was pacified. (verse 10)

Esther 8:1-8

147. The king gave Esther Haman's estate. (verse 1)
148. The king gave Mordecai his signet ring, which had once been worn by Haman. (verse 2)
149. Esther put Mordecai in charge of Haman's estate. (verse 2)
150. Esther fell at the king's feet and wept while begging him to reverse Haman's plan to kill all of the Jews. (verse 3)
151. Yes, he extended his scepter to her. (verse 4)
152. Esther asked the king to write a royal order that would override Haman's decree to destroy the Jews in all of the king's provinces. (verse 5)
153. The king told Esther that he had Haman hanged because he ordered the death of the Jews, and that he gave Haman's estate to Esther. Then he told Esther and Mordecai to write out a new decree and seal it with the signet ring he had given Mordecai, so that the new decree could not be rescinded. (verses 7-8)

Short Essay Questions

1. PART A: The first several verses state that God has a purpose for each of us, that we should share the Gospel with everyone, that God is preparing a place for us in heaven, and that our focus in life should be on God as opposed to gaining things for ourselves. The 1 Timothy and Titus verses refer specifically to guidelines for women. The verses from Revelation remind us that we're being prepared to live with God in heaven forever.
   PART B: Answers will vary.
2. Answers will vary.
3. The verses mostly refer to the negative consequences of pride; some also mention that God wants us to have a spirit of humility.

4.   Esther 1:12   Queen Vashti's refusal to come to the banquet, which led the king to look for a new queen (thus giving Esther a chance to become queen).

      Esther 1:19   The expert's advice that the king should look for a new queen.

      Esther 2:5-6   Mordecai (and therefore Esther) would not have been in Susa if Mordecai had not been taken into exile by the king of Babylon.

      Esther 2:8-9   Out of all the young women taken to the palace, Esther quickly became the favorite of Hegai, the keeper of the harem.

      Esther 2:16-17   Out of all the young women in the harem, Esther became the king's favorite and soon, his wife.

      Esther 2:21-22   Mordecai learned of the plot against the king and was able to tell Esther.

      Esther 5:2   The king held out his golden scepter and allowed Esther to make a request of him even though he had not called for her, which could have resulted in her death.

      Esther 6:1-2   The king couldn't sleep, asked to read the book of records of the chronicles, and learned that Mordecai had not been rewarded for saving his life.

      Esther 7:7-8   The king returned from the garden just as Haman threw himself at Esther, enraging the king and leading him to decree death for Haman, punisher of the Jews.

      Esther 8:2   The king gave his ring to Mordecai, giving him the power to rescue the Jews.

5.   No; as Mordecai points out, God could use someone else to save the Jews, but Esther and her family would not survive.

Esther